FOUR

FOUR

Call to Future Shepherds

Lifescape: Zero to Thirty-Two

Into the Future

The Walk

SHAUN DENOOYER

RESOURCE *Publications* • Eugene, Oregon

FOUR

Call to Future Shepherds, Lifescape: Zero to Thirty-Two, Into the Future, The Walk

Copyright © 2024 Shaun DeNooyer. All rights reserved. Except for brief quotations in critical publications or reviews, no part of this book may be reproduced in any manner without prior written permission from the publisher. Write: Permissions, Wipf and Stock Publishers, 199 W. 8th Ave., Suite 3, Eugene, OR 97401.

Resource Publications
An Imprint of Wipf and Stock Publishers
199 W. 8th Ave., Suite 3
Eugene, OR 97401

www.wipfandstock.com

PAPERBACK ISBN: 979-8-3852-0449-6
HARDCOVER ISBN: 979-8-3852-0450-2
EBOOK ISBN: 979-8-3852-0451-9

02/13/24

CONTENTS

CALL TO FUTURE SHEPHERDS | 1
  My Fantasy | 3
  Those Who Never Examine Themselves | 4
  A Great Man Sets His Sights | 5
  One's Soul May | 6
  What One Can Know of Another | 7
  There Is | 8
  Sacrilegious Desire | 9
  The More You Think | 10
  The Soul Is The Vortex of the Universe | 11
  Why | 12
  True Identity | 13
  The Growth of the Mind | 14
  In Another Time | 15
  That One Has Such a Malleable Form | 16
  Near Ghost | 17
  Note to the Space Traveler | 18
  Shade of Blindness | 19

Regarding Existence | 20

Having Been Given Such Weight to My Being | 21

Take Heed | 22

If the Heights That Thou May Reach | 23

Let Not, That Ye May | 24

That We May, We Must | 25

Untitled | 26

At the End of the Golden Reign | 27

Methinks | 28

Glimpse | 29

Ye Know Not | 30

Atop the Mountain of the Ego | 31

Origin of Nightmare | 32

Loiterer | 33

Soliloquy | 34

Unknowing Fugitives | 35

Woe That We Should | 36

We Are Not Yet Ill at Ease | 37

Rhetorical Question | 38

Ultimate Neglect | 39

Let There Be Those | 40

Diseases of the Heart May | 41

Such May Be | 42

Plea | 43

Question | 44

Eden Unfound | 45

The Gilded Throne | 47

Call to Future Shepherds | 49

LIFESCAPE: ZERO TO THIRTY-TWO | 51

INTO THE FUTURE | 99

   I | 101

   II | 102

   III | 111

   IV | 120

   V | 121

   VI | 123

THE WALK | 127

CALL TO FUTURE SHEPHERDS

MY FANTASY

My fantasy is for the god-caulk
In the cracks of my brain to expand,
Expunging me to the status of a
Prophet to where I stand on earth
As an old map.

THOSE WHO NEVER EXAMINE THEMSELVES

Those who never examine themselves shall end up moving
Throughout their days in a slur of detachment like the
Shadows of a spinning clock.

Are you disinterested in your life enough to be
Replaced with nothing like an apparition?

A GREAT MAN SETS HIS SIGHTS

beyond the Horizon

A great man sets his sights beyond the horizon
So as to be struck by the ebb and flow of a
Foreign tide, that he may, in a wave of doubt,
Discover a thousand sunken treasures.
Then there is the sailor of the sea of perfection—no swell
Unknown, no gust too strong—placidly gliding through this
Life but with the delusions of wondrous affairs.

ONE'S SOUL MAY

One's soul may stand comfortably naked, eternally
Replenished by the full scope of love, and though this truth
Sometimes seems not to make but a ripple upon the pool
Of consciousness, it exists everywhere about us.

Rather than to put thy heart on display like a robust
Piece of meat amongst ravenous wolves, 'tis to
Remain open to the possibility of its deepest function,
That one may find oneself within, what may have
Been thought of, at one time, to be
Out of the realm of reason.

WHAT ONE CAN KNOW OF ANOTHER

What one can know of another is
More than what the sea releases to the shore.
Therefore, 'tis not to stand by in the wake of a
Storm, but to set sail upon these waters
That ye may find wreckage upon
Unknown islands of further connectivity.

THERE IS

There is a state of Christian maturity in which
One (having become enveloped in the mystery
Of the Faith) is bestowed with true discernment,
Refining inquiry into the blossoming of a true vision,
Whereby, one cannot but give glints of heavenly matter.

SACRILEGIOUS DESIRE

The yearning of my being is too restless to be easily slotted
Into a manicured existence, thus 'tis not my wish to be
As an emperor transfixed by the shine of golden garments,
But a complete soul sharpening all manner of living
With the strength of my voice.

I've deepened the search within myself but to
Gain a greater aptitude to pursue the
Goings-on of the fullness of being.

Each step I take can be linked to the trek of
Every great man, yet as I am little more than a
Blur among a league of angels,
I am left having to make even more of an
Advancement on the blueprint of man.

Note: I shall increase identity to a new form,
To a new order of man.
I shall stand like a monument to naked existence,
Inlaid but with the most truth-stapling scars.

THE MORE YOU THINK

The more I love myself, the more you despair.
The more you think I have become something of
A completer being, the more you become
Enslaved to your grief.

My pain is the meat of your life,
And when you think I have reached
The pinnacle of my existence,
You will have turned into a bloodthirsty animal.

THE SOUL IS THE VORTEX OF THE UNIVERSE

The soul is the vortex of the universe:
A magnet for the horrendous matter of hell.
And those who remain unresponsive to such a reality,
By the magnitude of what's at play, will thus
Continue to be solely controlled by a rabid and
Wicked world, or, become ever detached from
Themselves, stormily drawn but into a
World of illustrious illusions.

WHY

Why dost thou make thy soul so sick and bitter?
Why dost thou hold thy tendencies to such vague expression?

Dost thou not know, that with thy Faith,
The dark water should ripple and scream?

TRUE IDENTITY

True identity is born in Christ.
Without him, what you think is
The true you, is actually the opposite
Of the you, you would be.
Thus, what you claim is the true you,
Is actually your archenemy.

THE GROWTH OF THE MIND

The growth of the mind happens like the
Blossoming anew of a withered tree, whereby
One must first extract the poisons of fruit overripe.

IN ANOTHER TIME

In another time you might have been the life prisoner
Of a king who kept you chained up in close proximity
Of criminals for their rehabilitation.
Present day tells us that you are bound by the
Chains of prior days, reaching no further
Than to lie in the bed of unrest.

THAT ONE HAS SUCH A MALLEABLE FORM

That one has such a malleable form,
And that we live in such a threatening climate,
One must learn further lest the fibers
Of thy being by such sinister spinners,
Turn to mere fluff, leaving one all but
At ease with all types of oppression
Like comfortable garments.

NEAR GHOST

Placidly, he goes,
Dully performing the tasks of daily life:
A tramcar existence unaware of the
Goings-on underground.

NOTE TO THE SPACE TRAVELER

The stars are a part of the buttoning-up
Of this plane of existence, and without the
Expansion of the experience of inner nature,
Outer nature becomes but a sterile atmosphere
And one goes to die in a wreckage of the cosmos.

SHADE OF BLINDNESS

I am too blind to see the
Growth of which I am capable:
That that may only come
Upon the clearing of immortality.

REGARDING EXISTENCE

If we should say that death, for those in Christ,
Unlocks the most sacred plane upon which
The soul rises to its immortal stature,
Triumphing to the affirmation of perfect beauty,
Leaving one but to begin one's travels throughout
The endless expansion of eternity,
Then let it also be said that such a miraculous
Endeavor, is, granted us solely by the birth of
Our previous existence, without which, such a
Sublime after would be lost but to the perfect before.

HAVING BEEN GIVEN SUCH WEIGHT TO MY BEING

Having been given such weight to my being, balanced
Only by my connection to, others of the like, I pursue
But those who are involved in similar disciplines.
For I am not like one who, like a bird, cares not
What grain is laid among the dirt as
Long as it be easy enough to swallow.
Nor could it satisfy me to quest but through
Endless expansion, able only to dive deep
But into the sterile waters of a creatureless ocean.

TAKE HEED

If the peace were to be broken within
A serious man, beware, for there is nothing
More threatening than an oncoming
Avalanche of a gargantuan soul.

IF THE HEIGHTS THAT THOU MAY REACH

If the heights that thou may reach depends
Upon the attachment of thyself to such
Escalating pursuits, and if thy aspirations are
Such but to tout thy glory; if ye continue
To climb in such a deceitful framework,
Ye will find such caustic depositing
Tarnishing thy soul, extinguishing thy heart,
And darkening thy mind.

LET NOT, THAT YE MAY

Let not thy success be determined by society,
But only by the divine telling of regeneration,
That ye may become a soul fully rid of that
Which, needless, needn't cling, thereby
Allowing acceptable thought to sweep
Through thy mind that steam may ye make
Of the vapor of time.

THAT WE MAY, WE MUST

That we've slit the throat of life, severing ourselves
From the natural order of our spirit.
That life seems to have boiled down to such
An insignificant practice, the movement of
Human progression such an aimless trajectory,
We must become aligned with the truth of ourselves,
That we may eventually achieve the completeness
Of being: the full representation of God's creation.

UNTITLED

Fruit unfathomably harvested
Amongst endless fields of rot.

AT THE END OF THE GOLDEN REIGN

At the end of the golden reign, on the threshold
Of the world, man walked into existence, whereupon
He fell to his knees, trembling amidst the darkness.
Feeling confined to the world like a restricted eternity,
Yet sensing his heart qualified for this plague-ridden place,
He rose to his feet, and with a step most sturdy and his
Soul ablaze, persisted further into the world . . . threatening
Friction upon the plane of unknowable answers.

METHINKS

The world at its most magnificent is
Man at his most prolific, and yet
Methinks the birth of a superman
May leave the world but to
Fall apart in his absence.

GLIMPSE

I have seen something
That would lessen the miraculous sightings that
Linger in the mind of a cosmic sailor.
I have seen something that allows me the hope
Of witnessing that of the grandest
Of spiritual gestures.

YE KNOW NOT

Ye know not the cause of the
Most universal woe.
For ye think the purpose of man is to
Reveal the god of the soul.

ATOP THE MOUNTAIN OF THE EGO

The seed of greatness lies within me
Bursting but with the growth of
Constant epiphanies, adorning my soul
With the rarest of human beautifications
To where I stand alone, sending my message out
Amongst a congregation of shadows.

ORIGIN OF NIGHTMARE

God created the world with the end of all things
In the eternity of his eyes.
On the seventh day, within the mind of this infinite being,
Swarmed the images of time.

LOITERER

Having shed his name in the night of another world,
Exempt of the duties of now, in pursuit of nothing,
He lolls about, ever satisfied astonishing
Our world with his timeless presence.

SOLILOQUY

I love without regret, seek without shame.
Am in constant pursuance of cracking the
Egg of the ego but to reveal the yolk of the soul.
Am constantly realigning myself to stay in step with
Another but for the grandest of soul-flourishing moments.
Am constantly seeking to iron-out the
Fractures of bygone faults.
To simmer the quake-birthing trauma
Of the suffering soul.

UNKNOWING FUGITIVES

We disguise our surrender in the guise
Of survival, spending our lives the slaves
Of the state of our heads.

No less than plentiful bounties
For the heavenly hunter.

WOE THAT WE SHOULD

Woe that we should eternally wade but in the
Shallow end of introspection, ever to be stranded
Upon the shore of a most dismal world, merely
Waiting out our lives but for those whose strides
Across this earth should ripen a new world, leaving mankind
To be found like the fossils of an old civilization.

WE ARE NOT YET ILL AT EASE

We are not yet ill at ease with, or seem to have no
Qualms about, the technological deity hovering
About us, surveying the stock of the soul.
For we passively submit to the progress
Of an anxious future: a persistent chaos gaining
Momentum upon the wafting-away of our souls.

RHETORICAL QUESTION

If the roots of humanity were to become cankerous
But with the growth of such poisons, that one were
Unable to drink their spiritual nutrients, what would
Keep the mind, the heart, and the hand, from
Becoming but a repertoire of caustic tools?

ULTIMATE NEGLECT

If the quest of man were to remain exterior,
The interior world, no longer sought,
Mankind would eventually be without
A trace of humanity, and thus shall become
A phantom race, eerily swaying to-and-fro,
All but conscious of a soul.

LET THERE BE THOSE

If the world were to become a most caustic realm,
And, that to take a backwards step, would be, to bear
In the heart a thousand transgressions, let there be those,
Who, amidst such horrendous conditions, are fearlessly
Taking on the pain and suffering of another, striving
To be but one of the strengthening stitches
Keeping whole the fabric of humanity.

DISEASES OF THE HEART MAY

Diseases of the heart may run the blood
And fill the veins, but dare I say that 'tis
Only from a prideful sediment
That a world of calamity may form.

SUCH MAY BE

Thrust upon the numbing wave of the
Tackling of reason whilst spliced together
With innumerable gifts of Glorification.
Such may be the process, for the Christian,
Of being strapped to one's eternal structure.

PLEA

Dear Lord with all thy grace, protect me
In this fallen place.
My backbone sturdy as a cane, yet
Still wobbly with no aim.
To the land of golden dreams, I do
Not halt but further lean,
To rest my frame in solemn grass and let
The winds of past time pass.
For I knew the scene of day that sparkled fine
Through work and play.
Of the land I walk today,
I ask by morn, be gone away.
Of my grief I do declare, 'tis the
Pain of might I wear.
Make thy way to the best, and put
This beast of mind to rest.
Of thy way I long to be
And crush my mind with mind of thee.

QUESTION

If we should live to see the devastating effects
Of the horror of a crumbling world (ill-equipped warriors
Draining themselves of their blood in lack of pursuit
Of another calling; bodies, plagued, retracting from their
Form into a twisted mess of protruding bones; the streets
Being lifted into the sky like a tidal wave of elephant skin;
Everywhere slowly becoming nowhere like the sky . . .),
Would the evils, lurking in the soul, stamp man with
A rotten seal, leaving one but with the freedom
Of a devil's wanderings, or would we stand steadfast
Against such horror, and part from this world
On a stride seldom taken.

EDEN UNFOUND

Rebelling against what they deemed a "sterile,
Passionless home," which they foremost thought to be
The most desolate chamber of despair, they hit the road,
Striving but to live in a paradisiacal realm of unbound
Existence, quickly becoming entangled in the heinous
Experience of make-believe freedom, sustaining themselves
On stealing sprees and random black-market dealings,
Evading reality by creating a fantastical realm
In which they reign supreme.

Having become absorbed in such topsy-turvy endeavors,
Leaving places in their souls dim enough to hide more of
Despair, many a night finds them mixing with the world
Seemingly enough to become momentarily immune to such a
Pervading sickness—recollections of the evening lost amidst
The acceleration of experience.

Longing to take part in an existence of more comfortable woes,
Yet no longer knowing the difference between safety and
Comfort, they find themselves melting into the arms of
Desiring strangers, giving themselves to the world in a
Loosely-wrapped gift of forgotten morals, their bodies
Making friends whilst their blindfolded minds fantasize to
The heights of a lobotomized state, with many a morning
Finding them in the awkward entanglement of human bodies
Encrusted with sexual liquid in the blistering sun—the shame,
Eating away at their souls like a mystical hive until the memory
Bank becomes but a hallucinatory realm of unaccredited data.

From the pressures of the day, to, the ruining of the night,

Retreating into their minds only to be thrust back into ever
Such a battering of everyday reality, stealing further and
Further into the territory of forgotten dreams (leaving
The repair of their souls to become all but an
Unfathomable task), they become hypnotized by
The strobe of the streetlights, hoping that 'tis
But the signification of alien abduction.

THE GILDED THRONE

Let it be said that there are those whose souls
Are swarming with the most wretched of human ills.
And others, making up what we shall call the indifferent,
Ever watching atrocities happen like a movie.
Let it thankfully be said that there are still yet those
Attune to the affairs of the heart, ever striving
As the mules of justice.
And let it be ecstatically said that there are others,
Having dwelt so long in the soil of artificial riches,
Having worn ever so proudly the rewards of the world,
That have come upon but the quest to purify their hearts.

But let it further be said, and reiterated, over and
Over again, that there are those who've been
Thrown away by the world, ever roaming the earth,
Never seeming to find from where they've been exiled,
Left but to rummage the bargain bins of love
On the outskirts of existence constantly vandalized by
Innumerable passersby, and those amongst them,
Who've come to believe that they'll never again be
Repaired in life, who've fallen to such a degree that
The smothering of their spirits has become but
The most comforting of blankets, and yet still others
Who cannot find release but in a catastrophe of the
Psyche, thus reflecting a world so completely desolate
That, seemingly even the greatest of harvests
Could not bring forth but a poisonous soup.

Man was not born ordained with the wings of
Preeminence, nor should it be his quest to gain

The crown of such an impious status.
Yet 'tis this very idea, this claim to the gilded throne,
That keeps one in constant judgment of another.
Therefore, unless we vanquish from our minds such a
Preposterous notion, we should find evil coming to such a
Boiling within us, leaving us to
Despair over the burden of our hearts.

CALL TO FUTURE SHEPHERDS

If it should come to pass, that fear was to catch hold
Of the brain like a frozen sponge, we may come to see
Many a soul all but throw away their humanity, pursuing
A life of survival with the eyes of an animal.
We may see many a determined eye become but a stagnant
Pupil cocooned in a bald nest, and the beards of old wise men
Become heavy with sweat like the coats of lost lambs.

We may see many, closing themselves off from the center
Of the city, venturing towards the deepest of valleys trying to
Locate geographically what they feel breaking inside, and
Many others who seem to have been released from the
Grip of sanity like a fighting cock.

We may see many striving to protect themselves by
Systematically forming gangs out of a rundown ensemble
Like reworking a worn-out quilt with strong patchwork,
And many others by any means necessary severing themselves
From the debilitating attachment of the earthly umbilical cord.

Note: if the human race were to become, by the plague of fear,
Sorely disconnected, leaving many a soul but solely driven
Toward one's own destruction, we may thus see the world
Become but a free-range pen of suffering animals in which,
Sheep are the primary target.

LIFESCAPE
Zero To Thirty-Two

As I look back, making my way through my memories as if lost in the murkiest of places, I find myself pressed upon the idea of the origin of my birth as being no less than the hand of God lifting me out of the swallows of the abyss and over the roaring waters of the before-birth domain, cupping me high in the palm of His hand, and with a rushing thrust . . . into this breathing world, absorbed by my mind like the dreams of a prophet. Day one found me housed in an incubator. My body remarkably still like standing water. My parents stood firmly about me through the passing of night, adding a rare shade of warmth to the light of the morning. Is one truly bound if one could never take flight? I eventually came through this early hardship blooming with a healthy color that seemed to be swarming with the promise of betterment. My birth was noted throughout the earth by the bearers of goodwill, unleashing a flurry of sparks from the bombastic movement of their torches like a rare breed of fiery insects. It wasn't long until my eyes ran wide, and my head began to sweep (how miraculous it is that a newborn baby with blink-less eyes might register the sights of the world as but a vision of innumerable wonders). My formative years remain somewhat vague, but I do remember feeling the discontent of a restricted existence bound to a static union. In my universe, mother was an unexplored planet and father, the sun, totally eclipsed. Our world is a world among worlds, and as I was to grow up as a privileged inmate, it was only through adventurous imagination and fantastical escapism that I was not hopelessly bound as the actions of shadows. My world consisted mostly of two parents and a sister, grandparents also, yet further so, and relatives, loosely round. As much love as my mother showed me, for which I'm ever thankful, the religious aspect was quite stern. Let it be said that a child is not concerned with the rhetoric of sheepish adults or, over what rules to follow. O how wondrous and frightening it is that one learns most how to live during the most impressionable and vulnerable time of his life (having to automatically catalogue memories), especially since the child is, earthly speaking, the foremost designer of this majestic cloth. My father is a passionate man, but because of his emotional handicap, I've been kept from really knowing anything about him. He is as closed off as the leper is from society, the obvious difference being the leper's disease is external, but the internal feelings, I would imagine, are quite similar. I don't know how much of my father's emotional disease was brought on by the damages he experienced growing up, and how much of it is self-inflicted. Whatever the answer, there's still no progression. Sentimental movie scenes bring him to an uncontrollable outpouring of tears. I don't know if the heart holds the blueprint for the soundest of infrastructures, but I do know that the mysterious fiddling of the heart needs to be deciphered to strengthen one's connection to oneself and, thus the world. His heart, because of the lack of the daily flow of emotion, is not able to exude its longings in any regular form of behavior, and thereby manifests in outlandish emotional outcries (babies and youngsters cry because they cannot express what they feel, want, and need. Likewise do adults cry because they are not being heard). I remember him getting very emotional over the Super Ted television cartoon. The show was about a stuffed teddy bear that was deemed defective and was tossed into the garbage, but then came back (with the help of an alien) as Super Ted. I think the reason for at least part of this sentimentality is that when I was born, I was borderline mentally retarded. My mom's mom is a very tender soul whose love and gentle touch could revitalize the most woebegone soul. She gave what she could for the upkeep of others. The nearer I was to her, the more revitalized I felt. I would go as far as to say that I even breathed better in her presence. I think her kindness and gentility helped me grow in a most thorough way, for she brought to my life a kind of homey affection. The guidance she gave me was not the guidance of the wisdom of thought but was a kind of sagacity borne of the dimension of the heart. She is one whose heart could be studied by science as a tool for the advancement of man. My mom's dad, I'm told, also had a robust heart, but he had a stroke when I was around ten, and I don't remember the way he was before it. I'm told that he would let my mother, in winter, use their only car to go to Bible study, and that he would take the bus (transferring three lines) to get to work. I remember my mom's dad as a docile creature who was constantly frustrated over not being able to get people to understand what he wanted: he would look at me, and then with his dominant hand point a couple fingers whilst saying the word here over and over again to get my attention for something that he wanted, and I would guess and show him things until either I succeeded in getting him what he wanted or until he began to quietly seethe over my lack of success. My uncle (one of my mom's brothers) is a gentle, big-hearted man who happens to be schizophrenic. This uncle of mine is a man who best represents those who are seemingly passed over by the traditional forms of fate, leaving him a kind of freedom lost to the rational thinker. He speaks with the delivery of one who sees his time worthy of a slow delivery. He answers questions with the thoughtfulness of one who has had time to think. And he always gives a sincere answer to a sincere question. He is a God-believing man but does not answer religious questions as if he didn't have a mind open to the exploration of thought. My dad's dad seemed a cruel man. He always made me nervous. I felt uneasy sitting close to him. To even look at him was quite disconcerting, but not because his face resembled a lion masterly worked into the mold of a human, but because he was an intense, woe-laden man, a wily soul swarming with an insecurity that was masked by the temper of a fabled beast. The tone of his voice was harsh, and when he spoke, his words rumbled out like the notes of a primitive music. He had warmth, but 'twas difficult to know when and where it would show. My dad's mom was similar in that she too had a bristly way of being. She moved like a spirit unable to transcend the confinement of blood and muscle. It was quite enough to be standing next to her. She too had warmth, but like a sun running through a biting climate. I didn't know how, or what to say to either one of them. They told. You did. I remember escaping the boredom (and the frightful anticipation) of the two-hour drive to my dad's parent's house by imagining, outside the window a small, slender, alien thing running alongside the car which I would make jump (by imagining) all along the man-made structures. I remember, upon arriving, quietly venting my frustration into my mom's ear at having to be there. Pre-dinnertime was spent watching the football game (the only time the four of us were at my dad's parent's house was on Thanksgiving or Christmas). I would sit uncomfortably quiet, watching the television. Sometimes, to keep from uncomfortable silences I would click my tongue in conjunction with the second hand of the clock. And I did this to remain inconspicuous, for without something seemingly capable of drawing my attention I would draw attention to how uncomfortable I was, and I never wanted that to happen. After the kitchen and dining room were cleaned up (sometimes I would help wash or dry the dishes. And even if I wasn't helping, I liked to stay in the kitchen because that's where my dad's dad wasn't) I would, to keep from interacting with anybody, act as though I was watching with great curiosity the nimble fingers of my aunt performing an abundance of needlework. What I remember most about growing up was saving money and going to church. I remember that Saturday mornings were usually taken up with the cutting out of coupons. And I remember going to church twice on Sunday with many a summer night having to fight to stay awake amidst the drowsiest of Sunday evening services. One of the best things I can say about this routine of beating Christ into my heart is that no matter what troubles I experience in this life I could never leave this world via the route of suicide. I soon became a most reverent disciple (more of a disciple to my mother than to Jesus) whilst simultaneously staring upward at God like an abandoned child. Let it be said that church may help stabilize a child, but cannot, of its own accord, properly rear him. I remember, one Sunday after church, in the food court in the mall (our Sunday lunch routine), after eating my slice of pizza, going into the arcade where I became exposed to a runaway child. This boy told me not to tell anyone that he didn't have a home. I was stunned. The world opened. I remember thinking that he must have been designed like an outlaw or that he had come of age by way of some special knowledge or that he had something sacred insulated in the interior of his heart. In truth, he had probably had his fill of the soup of despair. Most Sunday afternoons were taken up with driving around the city, going to Open Houses. A hobby of my parents and a drag for me. For what fun is it constantly walking through other people's homes to see but that which you didn't have? The only memory I have of my early schooling was when I was in kindergarten (or maybe it was preschool). I was waiting in line (as we all had to) for a drink of water and, this blonde girl I liked gave up her place in line because she wanted to wait next to me. I don't know why I remember this scene amidst all the other early-school memories I seem to be forsaking, but I do. At this time in my life, I had a couple good friends, and a spoiled neighbor-friend that lived behind us that I used to play with. This neighbor kid had a tall, well-constructed wooden play fort. It was fun to go up on the roof and, exhilarating to jump off into piles of woodchips. My own play fort was a place where loneliness began to scope out my soul—loneliness may lead to coldness, making connectivity a risky affair. I remember, between time spent at my play fort and secret hiding spots, going into wooded areas where I would imagine the soul-ghosts of whole families floating across the tops of trees, delightfully rising to heaven: I didn't think that the world was a bad place, I just thought that heaven was a better one. Sometimes, at night, I would sit under the suburban streetlights (the most forgotten place in the world), peering into the darkness at the end of the street, sensing that the future reveals itself to one at a most costly price. It wasn't long until I began to want to live in a forest. The idea of living deep within a forest was, to me, quite an enchanting one, as the world of the forest seemed to hold all things, especially the Black Forest of Germany (probably because its name seemed evocative of a fairytale). I wanted to live in a hideaway that kept me well hidden whilst at the same time seemed to be ever expanding (which is sometimes the effect in a large forest). Anything that began and then, without word, eventually stopped, made quite an impression on me (saddened me very much). Be it no more prayers at bedtime or the eventual end of an Easter basket. These things always left me bewildered to the point that I began to think that my parents had forgotten what they were supposed to be doing. "Toy time" for me consisted of sliding out the piano bench just so, and then choosing from my gray rectangular crate, which Ninja Turtles or Ghostbusters figures I would fight with. I would rarely play with my action figures with other kids, as I didn't like the way they would hold their figure by its whole body, and then begin smashing their figure against its enemy without any strategy. I preferred making my figures fight in a realistic way: I would hold one of the Turtles in one hand, and one of the other figures in the other, and proceed to control the fight in a methodical, slow-motioned manner until I decided which figure was going to lose by being driven to their death by falling off the edge of the piano bench, thus totally justifying the figure's death. I never agreed with the kids who would declare death on a figure merely by being hit (the figure wouldn't look any different). I thought it a faulty idea that one could, with no wherewithal to do so, just say that your figure was dead as opposed to having a viable reason for its death: someone merely telling you what the truth is when there's no truth behind it. This is why I always preferred to play with my toys by myself. The world gives us four distinct seasons (at least it did where I grew up), and each season is its own exhilarating world. My favorite time of year was winter. I loved sunny winter days. Loved perfect weapon-making snow, which I also used to make half-mad snowmen. I loved sledding too. Loved lifting into the air off large, near-frozen mounds and crashing into the trees of the woods. But most of all I loved Christmastime (still do). I remember, on Christmas Eve one year my sister telling me that she had seen Santa Claus and his reindeer outside her window the previous Christmas Eve, and that I should sleep in her room if I wanted to see what she'd seen. I believed that I was on the verge of witnessing an overwhelmingly awesome sight. I imagined that to see Santa would be like witnessing a dream become how clothing becomes on a body. It's difficult for me to think of anything in my childhood that I've anticipated as much as the prospect of seeing Santa and company. I cannot help but think that the child's everyday experience can include a form of rapture not unlike an artist or prophet. But what does it mean when, what one anticipates most is mere make-believe? I didn't know what MTV was until I was in sixth grade, as I grew up solely listening to the jukebox in our basement. The jukebox was full of Motown music, along with some Buddy Holly, Beach Boys, Johnny Mathis, Johnny Cash, Madonna, and others. One of my Saturday morning chores was to dust the basement. This was when I would listen to music. The quality of sound the jukebox gave off would be referred to, I guess, as low fidelity. Strong bass in a song rattled the machine like the slug of a baseball bat. I remember, once, going with my dad to look at jukeboxes at a house in Detroit. The man that had one for sale, my dad had told me, was called "Jukebox Bob." This man lived at home with his mother in a rather typical looking house, but all four walls of his mother's basement were lined with jukeboxes emitting a plethora of colors all curiously swirling into a most magnificent scene as if at the instruction of a maestro of an orchestra of light. From the day I was born until I was almost thirteen, three hundred and sixty-five days a year, until the summer before I started seventh grade, I wet the bed. I remember being petrified at the thought of spending the night at a friend's house, as I would inevitably wake with wet stinky clothes and a head full of innumerable excuses as to why there was such a foul smell in the air and why the ground was wet. Let it be said that a sleeping bag does not have the same absorbency as a maxi pad. Rolling the sleeping bag up barely covers the stench. And it wouldn't even have mattered, especially since my clothes were so thoroughly drenched. I remember, whilst staying at a friend's house (my parents were going out of town), being panic-stricken at the sight of the massive, navy-blue circle amidst the sky-blue sheets. I covered up the sheets with the comforter, put my pajamas in the hamper, took a shower and never mentioned it lest my shame withdraw me into hiding like a flower in winter. The worst of my bedwetting experiences was when I was on my sixth grade, end-of-elementary-school summer field trip. We slept in bunk beds lined closely together like an old-time jail. And since we were all so close together, in the morning somebody would inevitably say, "What's that smell?" And all I could say was, "I don't know, but yeah, that stinks." My dad owned quite a few handguns and, a rifle or shotgun as well. I remember going with him to buy some guns from a man who had curly gray hair and wore a green-and-black-checkered flannel. Pine trees covered his property, and his driveway went quite a ways back. My dad and my sister and I used to shoot the handguns in our basement. My dad would set two hefty phonebooks stacked one in front of the other in an upholstered chair. We would use shooting earmuffs, and every time we fired, I wondered if the neighbors could hear us (of course they could. You don't shoot a high caliber handgun in the basement of a house in the suburbs and not hear it), and if they could, what they were thinking. My world nearly stretched to the four corners of a square mile. I was frightened of the area of the neighborhood near the wall that stood at the back of the parking lot of the mall, for it seemed, to me, the territory of the shadow people continually bloating themselves back and forth into the world by sucking the poisons of the blackest of flowers. For me, childhood was both a delightful plane of creative glory and the most vacant station of existence like a waterless planet. Nature was kind of appealing to me. Not only do I remember being attracted to the exoticism of long grass and unbridled shrubbery, I sensed the birds sensed another world. I used to walk home from school, sometimes feeling estranged from my surroundings as if time had thought me not worthy of the future. Sometimes I felt that I had been forsaken, that my street was a part of the past and that my house was not my home, but merely where I was supposed to go. I remember, once, feeling very relieved in the wake of a midday thunderstorm. I felt, amidst such a massive, all-encompassing cloud of darkness, comforted by the way the world seemed to have lessened its way. I felt that I had been blessed with an out-of-time experience, a period of grace where the frenzies of my heart seemed to all but disperse, leaving me feeling like I had a place in the world. Every now and again there was a sighting of a man that looked frighteningly real, as if his soul had been forced into foreclosure, as his presence seemed to resemble a stone statue unable to take the wishes of charity. This was a man that seemed so worn out by the world (how much does one have to know of the world until they're made to carry the heftiest baggage?) as to become regarded as something too real to be looked upon, a frightening rarity of humanity, a relic of human creation. For some reason I felt fortunate to have observed this man. I felt that I had gained some kind of sacred knowledge. For this experience gave me the impression that the rest of the world wasn't real, but that only his experiences were. I soon began daydreaming about what I thought to be the lives of the people who lived where love resides (I felt that love was that which succeeds in eternally guarding against the demise of our souls). It wasn't long until the fancies of my mind became but a most enriching world: I would travel (in my mind) the outskirts of existence proposing that the proprietors of the golden realm bring me into their world like baby Moses snatched up from the Nile River. I wanted God (my real father) to welcome me in and give me a tour of my real home. I wanted to know where I came from. I wanted to see the beauty of heaven, and all the delightful things that I was missing. I wanted to hear my before-birth angel friends call me for fun by my self-appointed earthly nickname, "Bastard Angel." I merely wanted to hug my real father. For I yearn to know fully, He who is the maestro of the orchestra of the cosmos. A lot of my time was taken up with riding my bike around the neighborhood trying to build my thoughts up enough to be able to spout off ideas that could be considered enlightened. I think that some of my curious solo adventures stemmed from the lack of a much-needed partner in crime. The games I had to play to be liked, when I lost, told me that I wasn't worth the prize. I have been, most of my life, in close correspondence with the spirit of cowardice. I had a dream once where, amidst many unrecognizable people a family was joyfully splashing, and nearby, in a turbid mesh of sand and brush there was a child occupied with a focus that seemed to hold the seed of outlandish obsessions. It wasn't long until I began the routine of slowly facing the mirror in the bathroom, mouthing my worth to myself like a pre-show dressing room. It wasn't long until I began daydreaming about my future celebrity status. I began to long for a kind of fame that would come in the fashion of an insurmountable legion of fans. With such ignorant yearnings on the verge of becoming but an inescapable fantasy, I would sneak away from home and stand under the crude yellow glow of a streetlight in my neighborhood, momentarily taming my wistful desire for the limelight: I wanted to be famous, O so famous, but never wanted to become immersed in the delusional affairs of mass-market appeal, nor become over lit in the toxic rays of the limelight, stuffed with such poisons and thus full of such sickness that I should be left but grooming and doting like the supreme vanity of the sole inhabitant of a room of a hundred gilded mirrors. Feeling detached from what I felt was a most suspicious, even irrational universe I quickly fell under the spell of movies, enchanted by the idea that something "unreal" could hold something so meaningful. In the dark, within the glaring light of the television screen, the cinematic world came rushing into my soul, exposing me to rhythms of life I had yet to be exposed to. I looked to these moving pictures to understand the way that life could be lived. In some way I felt that these powerful images and fascinating ideas were but the makings of the actual reality of the world. Sometimes I would become ever so lonely as to think that people didn't exist, but by the mere fact that a real person had been in front of a recording camera, I knew that they did. In my loneliest moments it relieved me to know that I could go to the world of the cinema and know that there were many other people with all kinds of experiences. That it was possible to live all kinds of ways. I must admit that at this time in my life I was utterly fascinated by celebrities, or rather, by the celebrity lifestyle. I was fascinated by the fact that many a celebrity was usually seen, in the glossy still frames of celebrity magazines, meandering about looking good, seemingly going here and there without worry (I had a crush on Angelina Jolie, which began after having seen the movie Hackers when I was sixteen or seventeen. My bedroom was plastered with magazine cutouts, among them, Jolie being a prominent fixture: I had pasted a few pictures of her from the Rolling Stone spread she did (the issue with her on the cover with the sultry, pouty expression). In one of the pictures, she's posing with a most contrived sneer, holding a pint of some kind of liquor in one hand, a cigarette in the other, and her nipples, ever so slightly showing through her feminine wifebeater. A sight my mother covered over with black magic marker. I still laugh at my mother's love, so tight, yet still capable of being so giving. Winona Ryder was another, whose image I often held as the fully realized female beauty. I saw her physical appearance as classical beauty having been thrown down the chute of modernity). I was truly curious about the lives of celebrities, but I was not unaware of the artificial world that many a celebrity seemed to be inhabiting, which was ever so surpassingly fascinating in its wretched evocativeness, an unreal world in which the dreams of the heart are seldom pursued, to where one may take to such a withering that one is unable to withstand the scrapes of the psyche. Because I can empathize with those who relish in praise (either because they want to be seen as important or, possibly because they want to compensate for lack of talent or, that of not knowing themselves), I therefore have pity for the lives of many a celebrity. For me, the tragedies of many of these lives took on a most dramatic appeal, for 'tis only from such an unreasonable height that one may fall to the depths of despair. Let it be said that without ever having established one's identity, one may become engulfed in a life of exaggerated importance, and thus may find himself in a place where he no longer hears or is, able to make out, the whisperings of the soul. An existence having become as directionless as a fish unable to make even the most familiar dart, moving about seemingly without the need to exist, becoming like chum for the monsters of the abyss. When I became the ready age, sports became a huge part of my life. I think the first sport I was involved in was tee ball, which, as far as I can remember, went very well (I had fun). When I got a tad bit older, I had to be forced into playing softball. And not unlike many children who are sometimes spastically brought to tears at the thought of doing something new, such was the case with me. I was crying and pleading not to have to go. All I had to do was walk to the end of the street and ask for the coach of my team. But 'twas not necessarily this simple act that had me so emotionally ballistic, 'twas the fact that I would have to try to meet and greet amidst a sea of already-chummy baseball pals. Eventually I went through with it and became wildly excited about softball because of all the fun I experienced on that first day. Such an experience (merely figuring out how to do something by myself) brought me so much further into the world and thus excited me to such a degree that I couldn't wait to go back. This experience helped me to be a little less scared of new situations. It helped shift a little bit my perception of the world, merely by having done something that I had previously seen as but forced participation into the unknown region of the social nightmare (although there was no real danger). Just around the corner was football and basketball, real baseball too, the world of the sandlot. My heart thumped a rabid beat for sports. I think playing team sports could have a profoundly positive effect on the development of a child. Let it be said that a "nobody" may become a hero on "the field," like an important figure in a most fascinating mythology. Elementary school was kind of a difficult time, as I didn't make friends that easily. I did, however, have a couple friends, and during recess, at least in the beginning years of my elementary school experience I would, with one of these friends, journey into an imaginative landscape in which we called ourselves Blue Fighters (I don't know why we called ourselves that). I had fun exploring this world, as it was a thriving creative bubble made up of our own making, where the plagues of the world surrounding momentarily drowned out, including the off-putting sounds of the misguided strides of malicious action (there were a couple of older boys who used to terrorize me when I was by myself by chasing me around the playground), where one feels like one's own self whilst simultaneously feeling eerily unspoken for like a soldier born on the field by the choice to fulfill his duty. I can't firmly recall when it was that I began to play sports at recess. And I don't remember if I had to become accepted into playing sports with the other boys, or if I had just decided one day to start playing. What the girls did, I don't recall. I was better at football than most of them would admit. I could run fast and could, for the most part, catch what was soaring about me. Football was fun, but basketball was my sport. If the other kids weren't that fond of me playing football, and a few were quick to tell me so, basketball was where they shut their mouths. They kept quiet mostly because they didn't want to say something that would immediately backlash into an embarrassment fully legible upon their faces as if having gotten in the way of a novice prep cook trying to prepare a delicacy primarily involving beetroot. In the lunchroom, to impress my lunch mates, I would make my face beet red. It was a ploy to draw attention to myself. It was a hey-look-at-that-weird-kid-he-can-do-something thing. I remember going on a field trip to I don't know where, but clearly remembering sitting next to a girl (we were carpooling) with shorts on. I was wearing shorts as well, and as the back seat was full, our bare legs were touching the whole way. This was a most wonderful feeling. Even though there was nothing said, and though she may not have even liked me, such an occurrence made me feel that the world had good things to offer, especially since it was an occurrence in which I had no part in orchestrating. My first kiss (I think it was my first) was had with a girl my mom used to babysit (watch before school). This happened in a swimming pool in a Holiday Inn (her dad used to take us there). I remember her wrapping her arms around me, and then quickly pulling her body to my chest to give me a tight-lipped kiss. What I remember most about middle school was that I was bullied a lot, and that I had to hurry home after school to record General Hospital for my mom. Middle school was also the last time I would see an A on one of my report cards. It was about at this time in my life that I began to see my neighborhood as quite dreary, even cheerless. A fantasy of mine at this time was to become lost in the hustle and bustle of the main drag of a major metropolis. A suburban community is, often a large-scale hideaway for those who've given up on life, and when I saw many a family "being together," I saw but the disturbing poses of the members of families seemingly detached from their lot. If there was but only a curb to determine the edge of the artificial turf of our society! Woe to the pseudo connections of delusional families! Youth soon became such an eerie period for me that I began believing that the place I was in was not the place that I should be. I would constantly try and think of another time and place to inhabit. But how does one escape from the prison of time itself? Sometimes, in the stillness of the night, sensing that the world was telling me that I should be doing something other than what I was doing, I would look into the looking glass to see if I resembled who I perceived myself to be, then go outside, scope the land and think about making a go at trying to live a different life (I longed to breathe the air of mythic America: decrepit bridges were much fodder for my imagination, for they seemed to me what was left of the elaborate structure of a fully connected land), and yet I would get nervous at the thought of having to live a wholly different life than I had been living, to where I would end up spending my days, patiently existing, waiting upon the gift of transformation. In some way I felt that I had to discover a divergence from the path of the child lest I become a continual child, playing a game, the rules of which, leave the player profoundly misguided. I don't know if I was ever at ease with the way my soul was ingesting the world. Even as a child I felt childhood passing away, which was quite unfortunate as childhood is the richest, most human-forming time of existence, the privileged yet sensitive time in which the foundation of the human mold quickens to the majority of its final structure. It wasn't long until I became what I would refer to as a hypothetical person, as I seemed invisible, removed from my species, displaced amidst the herd, lost in time. A child's outings and adventures are but delicious follies yet to be accompanied by threatening storms, and delinquency was right around the corner. My first automobile was a moped. I would drive around town, holding up traffic. I had no reason to ride a bike anymore, and anyway, rusted or unused bicycles had become a depressing sight, giving me the impression that the way of the child becomes entirely lost in the realm of adulthood. This moped was the only form of transportation I used. I was suddenly capable of quickly getting to the girl's house I was fond of at the time. It was tough riding in the wintertime, but what is a little discomfort and careful riding compared to not going somewhere that I had previously not been able to go to, or, had not been able to go to as quickly as I wanted. You could go anywhere if you had a little gas money and a bit of endurance. When I was about fifteen (freshman year of high school), there was a girl I liked (the one I used to visit on my moped). We hung out a little bit, sat in the driveway, whatever. We went, once, to a renaissance festival (at her request). I bought her a candle that cost twenty dollars. I remember that when people found out (her circle of friends) how much my candle-gift to her was, laughs ensued. I remember writing the girl I liked a letter that I no doubt must have thought was, at the time, just a sincere telling of my feelings. But to look back on it, 'twas no doubt a profound exuding of my utter lack of self-worth. If I recall, the letter had a sentence in it that said something like this: *I would never think that a girl like you would want to be with someone like me.* The assignments I had to do in high school, I felt, were more than laborious. I didn't understand any of it. It couldn't have been more alien. I did next to no work. I tried in the beginning but ended up barely doing any in any class except when someone would let me cheat off them, if you can call that work. Or did the work of merely shading the bubbles of multiple-choice questions just to go through the motion of doing what everybody else seemed to understand doing so that I wouldn't be singled out as one who would have to give answers as to why he wasn't doing it. Such a frame of mind tends to dream, or at least tends to think about what is going on outside the class. Coming upon a good teacher in high school is like an angel infiltrating a diabolical realm, but it does happen. There wasn't a class (sleeping room) I enjoyed, although there were two teachers I liked. One of these teachers once wrote me a note that said: *You're gifted at making excuses/just don't make too many/remember the little people when you become a star*. I had another teacher that let me turn in homework up to a week late with no penalty. He knew that I was struggling and just wanted me to be able to get the work done, and turn it in. I failed his class but appreciated his grace. These two teachers made an indubitable impression on me. It wasn't long until I stopped bringing report cards home. The more I became detached from the academic world (such as it was), the more I became involved in exciting, albeit mischievous activity: (I was hollow enough to be filled with a most devilish fodder) we (me and an acquaintance of mine) would light off fireworks in the bathroom: we would wrap the wick in toilet paper, light the toilet paper and then walk away. We had about fifteen to twenty seconds to feel relaxed enough to get into a normal-type walk on our way into the lunchroom (I think that the birth of rebellion in me was the first step in recognizing the gravity of one's soul). I remember, one time during finals week, having had some liquor at a friend's house before school, taking my First Hour exam, when suddenly the power went out, and when the teacher left the class, I crawled outside the window, acting like I had to pee in the courtyard, then came back in via the courtyard door. This was just a way to get a few laughs from my classmates and the kids peering out the windows across the way. School was a place safe enough to do things that you couldn't do at home. The problem was that you would inevitably be caught, because, you had to go back. I disliked school, yet I had to go. This kept me constantly running. It was about at this time in my life when I began huffing gasoline, smoking heaps of weed and, consistently started drinking. It wasn't long until I was evading high school by way of the LSD escape route. And it wasn't long until I was skipping school altogether. I felt that school was too difficult, and besides, I was more interested, almost violently so, in being able to exhibit a grin that spoke of experience. It wasn't long until I let drugs slip into my life like the forming of trust in the beginning stage of a sincere friendship. I romanticized drugs. Growing up I thought that drugs were only used by the noblest of souls, the rebels, the infinitely inwardly gazing. My ignorance fed my devils, bringing me to fall twofold from the world of earnest strivings. I had come all the way from the closing of the curtain on the dramatics of childhood to, spending most of my time waiting to exit the uncomfortable vapidity of the day to release myself to the freedom of the drama of the night. The major bother was always the day after, having to make it through the sickness of the morning to reach the comfortable alcohol setting of the evening. My soul came to devote itself to the vocation of dependency. Many a dawn would I return home with many a bruise of the midnight fall. Life at hand was so difficult to navigate that I began to build my own notion of the world in which I wanted to live: I would try to get one to three jobs a week, go for orientation, then never go back. This allowed me to get, every week, a three or four-hour paycheck from each job, allowing me to turnout enough money to ride out the week without really having to work, thus facilitating a life of fun: spending-money and long stretches of free time. But 'twas hard to maintain such a routine. Sometimes during my jobless stretches my mother would give me five dollars to go out for the evening. With this I would buy a 40 oz beer (two to three dollars) and either two Junior Whoppers, or a grilled cheese. At this time in my life, I had a zero-course appetite, and the prospect of filling my belly was but a sickening delight. It was about at this time in my life when I began to don a most disheveled appearance. And I had an air of arrogance that surpassed even the tabloid-driven celebrity. The looks people gave me were the kind they wished would hide me away. My behavior was becoming a most caustic display of a fettered mind (I remember, with a friend of mine, doing drunken donuts on the muddy white blanket of my former middle school football field in the middle of a snowstorm. And I remember, in the summer, during school hours, tearing up the well-groomed lawn out front of my high school. Does one fall so that they may enter into the freest form of expression?), and yet I still strove to hold onto the virtue of kindness, for 'twas the only thing that I felt could keep me in line with the daily to and fro of humanity. Even though I was becoming, in many ways, a very crass person, I always tried to be a sincere human being, for I thought that that was the most important thing to be. I thought that if I was sincere then nobody could find anything wrong with me. I thought that being sincere meant that one was a truer person, that one was more real. That, if one was sincere, then it was possible that one could fully discover oneself. I thought that a sincere person was a very aware person. But what I initially failed to realize was that sincerity without conviction leads one to become self-important. In time, such a realization would help me become cognizant of deeper certainties. I was seventeen years old (a junior in high school) when I went on my Spring Break trip. The whole experience was extremely tumultuous, albeit quite exciting, particularly the experience one of my friend's and I had, beginning one morning at 3:00am: we took five hits of double-dipped acid, left our hotel room and began walking along the beach (we referred to this drug-induced venture as a search for the meaning of life) in what turned out to be an eight-hour journey. My hoodie and Ray-Ban aviator sunglasses became my most needed objects, for they shielded me from the horrifying sight of the sanity of a sober person. These inanimate objects undoubtedly helped me make my way through a world gaudily flashing its hellish dream all around me. It wouldn't be more than a month after Spring Break that I would be kicked out of school. A year and a half later I got my GED. The only thing that saddened me or that I felt a little regret about regarding the end of my high school days was the fact that the girls that had made it at least somewhat apparent that they liked me, and, that I liked too, I never got to know. Time spent with girls was sparse: I had had quite a few make out sessions, but rarely anything more than that. I had a girlfriend in high school for about a month (we had been friends for a while, though I don't know if we had anything in common besides sharing a locker). I remember, going to a Haunted House with her around Halloween. And when we were almost at the end of the tour, we began to kiss, and I put my hand on her breast. When I did so, I said, "Sorry, is this o.k.?" And she replied, "You can do whatever you want, you're my boyfriend." What she said made me feel good, and, at the same time, kind of regretfully sad, as I had always felt that I never had the right, or that it could be seen as taking advantage of someone. I never wanted to take advantage of anyone, and yet I didn't want to have to apologize for doing something that I felt was part of a mutual feeling. More than wanting to be swarmed by many a desirous female, I merely wanted a regular date with a girl. That was a dream of my youth. I never accomplished that. If one does not pursue, one may never know what may arise out of such a pursuit. I never went to a homecoming dance, nor did I know how to ask a girl to go, nor did I think that anyone would want to go with me anyway: I thought that girls had always thought of me as the very image of unworthiness, a person of minor significance. Scared to date, scared to dance, on prom night, I sat on my porch, thinking about how many people were doing such things, good experience or bad, that they might forever remember. The truth was that I was a kind of convict, bound to the falsest of prisons. I didn't understand that the decisions one makes, or doesn't make, confirms the truth about one's existence. If one takes no action, pursues nothing, one may find oneself drug down to a most bitter and fallen kind of depths, leaving the dreadful effect of regret to take hold. Do not bind thyself to the idea that you are a lesser being, bound to a lesser life. That you are a weaker soul or that you lack a destiny. Do not make a decision and then ask for assurance lest the world condemn you like an innocent man who becomes, in the eyes of the warden, guilty upon entering prison. I traveled a decent amount during high school, and even more so verging into young adulthood (in my opinion, this age would be from eighteen on). I remember going to Florida with a friend of mine and his family (my friend and I drove separately). I remember the nerve-wracking experience of trying to follow my friend's mom at 3:00am through the mountains in heavy rain. I remember waking up achy at dawn in the car in Florida (I think we were supposed to meet my friend's mom's sister or something) in quite an expansive parking lot outside a strange looking apartment complex that resembled a shady motel. I remember getting out of the car (my friend was still sleeping) with the intention of finding my friend's aunt's apartment door (I had no way of knowing where it was). I remember roaming the Holiday Inn-like halls of these sad living quarters and being quickly confronted by multiple street cats which rocketed me back to the car. After getting settled in, and having always wanted to go boating, and since we were staying on the Gulf of Mexico, and with my friend obliged to go, we went. We bought a kid's blow-up boat, took a cube of beer (thirty beers) and a beer bong and set off. The boat came with two oars, but one quickly got lost after we started to drink. I remember, at one point, when the boat was half full of water, all too clearly seeing about ten feet from us a tortoise whose head was as big as mine. And about two drinks later we both saw a fin that we hoped belonged to a dolphin. I remember, at a certain point, not being able to see the shore. And I think we eventually lost both oars. But thankfully we made it back (with the help of the tide). There was another trip a couple friends and I took on a Greyhound bus (also to Florida). We rode the bus for about forty hours until getting kicked off (the bus stopped for about an hour or so, so we went to a bar in town, and my friends and I each had one beer. When we went back to the rest stop, I jangled the handle of a candy dispenser hoping to get a few broken pieces, and while doing so, the bus driver walked up close to me and took notice of my breath and said, "You're not allowed to have any alcohol in your system while on a Greyhound bus"). We had to wait until the next day (we were forced to take a different bus) to continue the trip, so my friends and I got a motel room and then drank beer under a bridge in Alabama. My life revolved around drinking: drinking whilst sitting on a couch and watching TV at a friend's house. Drinking whilst sitting in a car and listening to music. Getting drunk in the parking lot of a movie theater (we would sometimes sneak in to see a movie, sometimes not). The better part of me was a drinking and drugging bystander to disgraceful creatures listening to each other's instructions on how to become sexually astute: they would cheer and toast each other on their sexual exploits, finding momentary release from the lack of their lives in the wretched reflex of groping the bodies of passersby like fleshy playthings, justifying their hapless sexual encounters as but the pushes of the blood of desire. I thought many to be crippled with what I would call the jailbird syndrome: every girl in view was but the greenest of grass to be "picnicked" upon. I knew that I didn't want to bear any resemblance to those belligerent, incurious creatures, yet still was I ever suckling the poisonous mammary of the mother of wretched affairs. The emptiness of my life was filled with hyped-up, vaporous moments that quickly disintegrated into many a sour activity. When I would go out for the night I felt as if I was merely "putting in my time," making my way through the happenings of the evening, such as they were, all the while looking forward to coming home to bathe in the nurturing light of the cinematic world. When I got home from the night's endeavors (most of the time extremely intoxicated) I would go straight to my collection of over five hundred VHS tapes, select one of my favorites (my first favorite movie was Point Break. I would say that between the ages of sixteen and seventeen I had seen it more than fifty times. At one point in my life, I could quote about ninety percent of it from memory. I was totally captivated by this film. My fascination with this film stemmed from what I saw represented in the character of Bodhi. I saw him as a true seeker, a soul who happened to use surfing as a way to put himself in line with the most hidden of spiritual impulses. I was attracted to his intensity and his sincerity. I was attracted to the way in which he would speak regarding what he believed. I think it was the type of film, and the type of character that I needed to be obsessed with at that time in my life. A few years later, American Beauty would replace Point Break as my new favorite. You could say I saw it more than once in the theater. My fascination with this movie was, in large part, due to the sincerity of the character of Ricky Fitts. I was drawn to the seriousness in which he would respond to a remark, question, or demand. And the "bag scene" was a watershed moment for me. In a few years, I would see Breaking the Waves, which was like experiencing the untying of the braid of a religious scar), then go into the family room, pop it in, grab some blankets and lay on the couch. Sometimes my mom would come into the room and sit snuggled up to my face, talking to me as if I had just come home from a church picnic. The proximity of my mother at these times made me cover up my face with the blankets like a child who pulls the covers over his head to guard himself from whatever monster he thought was at hand. Many a night I would, because of these occurrences, bury myself in blankets and lay toward the crease of the couch with my face firmly pressed against the staunch upholstery, quite satisfied to merely listen to a movie. If I was buried under enough blankets, and if no light or outside air could seep in, I was as content as an animal in its burrow. Many an afternoon, when either the hard blue sky of my mind would give way to a most threatening storm, or, having become torn by an elusive manner of suffering and, not knowing wherefrom this plague persisted, I would close my eyelids, shutting down the sensory earth ball (I felt that it was possible somehow through a glorious slumber or through some type of intense focus to make the truth of myself awaken and thus bring about a great cleansing of my being). Some nights, broke and alone I would wander the vacant parking lots of suburban gas stations, for I wanted a hideout, and it had to be a vacant public place where I could go through the messes of the day, a "public stage" where I could "speak to the world" ever so freely. Sometimes, fearing that I might be heard, I would express, with hard mime inflection interspersed with nicks of sound, the petals of thought swirling about my mind. This way of expressing my thoughts, feelings, and yearnings put me in such a sensitive and extraordinary mood that the grounds I was on seemed to be straddling reality and dreams, for I felt exposed to that which might be referred to as "active silence" or, "alive air." That that seemed to give the wind a kind of divine flair, or a kind of holy inarticulateness. For a mere breeze across my neck seemed to infiltrate my breast, and my mental state seemed at a greater height. This was the period of my life when I first felt truly aware of the critical state of the soul. These times alone with myself in the outside world were rare, as I was usually on my way to meet up with or, was waiting to be picked up by one of my friends so that the night could "begin." I had become acquainted with that which is granted to one involved in mass quantities of drugs and alcohol: a notion (ever so fleetingly) of absolute comfort with the world, that place where one is guarded from the harshest winds of life, where one is emptied of one's need for companionship like a kiss steadily blown as if from the goddess of oblivion, that place where one can feel close to being hugged, or not feel, that they've never truly been. Though my being was constantly being rolled over by the boulder of oblivion, it seemed that death continually fled from me like the retracting paw of a jumpy cat. Sometimes, in the throes of my blunderings, my numbness of being would leave me feeling but a tickle of remorse like a dinosaur riddled with bullets. I had always thought my heart to be the most sought-after of sacred meat, and yet I felt that it had somehow become ravaged to the stingiest of portions. It was as if my soul had become a host but for the development of a most horrendous disease. I got to the point where I couldn't feel enough to rid myself of the worm of despair, digging its way towards what felt like the decay of my soul, leaving my innards to become like a wilted flower (the deadening of a spiritual tree with but a thirst for worldly ornaments). I think at that time of my life a storm of growth would have flooded my senses, and, moreover, may have possibly added dangerous friction to the scheming of such a tottering mindscape. Not knowing the lengths to which I was choking my existence, I eventually became one of those souls ever loosening themselves of inner activity. Such were my experiences that many were my losses of self, like radiant jewels endlessly falling out of a worn-out pocket. The wreath of my worth had become hung up on the blankest of walls. I remember, amidst suburban backyard deck parties, bone-rattling junkies harkening to young ears (the full meaning of which, I'm sure, escaped me at the time) possibly out of empathy or a heartrending yearning for throwback simpatico. This was about the time when I began having a reoccurring dream, beginning with me lightly falling amidst a peculiar fog of what seemed a kind of choking atmosphere, landing softly in a marsh-like world that had the consistency of a newborn animal, wherefrom I ventured through a trail of mashed brush, carefully stepping to maintain my balance whilst witnessing grotesque life-forms squeezing and flexing their bodies through the bedding of the wet terrain. It seemed that I was the inhabitant of a false reality, a shadow of my real self, an apparition pulsing through the void. It was as if I was living below the surface of existence, or, had strode deep into the netherworld, for the actions of the people surrounding me became but the most esoteric of notions. The jeering way a stranger would sneak a glimpse at me made me feel like a freedom fighter in a newly imposed police state. Let it be said that my trail upon the earth as it were, rather than a steady coherent mark was becoming but an indecipherable smear. I was endlessly trudging through the murky waters of the deepening swamp of my psyche. I felt that I was being led to that place of innermost grief where invading nightmares ransack the palace of dreams. Thoughts are controllable, only by one's ability to digest them, and mine were like fearful killers roaming a desert landscape. I wanted my mind to maintain its appeal like the clouds, but I felt that I had lost that which was necessary for my being to properly guard from atrocity. I felt burdened to such a degree that I began to have the feeling that I had possibly released, within the darkness of my psyche, the evils lurking therein. A most threatening poison rises off the deadening of a most sacred matter. With a fear of the devil in the mirror and a pain in the heart like a circus sideshow, I began to want to live a life of isolation, endlessly picnicking upon the earth's most species-free terrain. I longed to become acquainted with but that which lay beyond. To be called to the farthermost moonlit crest at the edge of the world, wrapped up in a holy endeavor eternally lengthened by endless visions. For I felt that the peace within me was irrecoverably breaking. That that would be similar to the falling apart of the infrastructure of the world. I wanted away, into a world of ethereal chaos shimmering and sprouting in all its abundant wildness like the furthest reaches of Monet. I had begun to view all of nature as but a cover-up of actual life, and moreover, as the blotting out of the actual reality of the world. I began to think that every swarming thing of our physical world was but a deceptive material having been twisted out of the vein of true existence into the continual birth of the falsest of pictures. That that which surrounded me was but the manifestation of the illness of the universe: the spiritual rash of an unclean world. I remember, about at this time in my life, witnessing a vagabond-like gaggle of men running through the streets, yelling as loud as they could that they would give their lives to be needed by someone. When they began to sing, a most profuse poetry charged from their hearts: the songs they sang seemed to be but the most sacred of hymns. It was like witnessing the heavens opening up to slap the faces of the living dead. I spoke to these folk about the journey that they seemed to be consumed with. I spoke to them about their ideals to which they were fully devoted. Most of our interaction consisted of them asking me quite a few questions, some of which were riddle-like and some of which, I thought at the time, to be very odd but in a most extraordinary way. They asked me if I felt I was capable of remaining a "person" through the trials of life. And they asked me if I thought I was capable of untangling strangling accusations but to a comfortable slap of the tongue. If I thought that my feet were at work with a meaningless trod. If I felt like a ghost with the baggage of a soul. If I thought that an off-the-grid man would accompany a traveling businessman. If I believed that I was a master architect of another world. If I thought that one may be better able to contemplate one's existence away from others. If my musings found me losing myself between this world and the next like an angel fading in and out of the confinement of human makeup. If I thought that the sting of regret had already penetrated a-ways into my soul. If I thought that the pain of youth was a mere shadow of the catastrophe of adulthood. If I thought that talent helps harness the beast of the will. And they asked me if I felt I knew the truth of that which makes heavy the heart of man. They also spoke to me about the oncoming slaughter of the "time of the wolf." I had always thought that I had been bound to a terrain of wellness. That each step I took was but a step towards my own identity, and yet it seemed that my footing had taken to a most directionless path. In every establishment I frequented, I'd notice myself looking out the windows pondering what other people were doing, ever curious about what made up the days of the rest of humanity. On top of being a lost hanger-on, backwardly flourishing like an ambitious villain, it didn't help that I was extremely self-conscious about my face: I wanted every surface to resemble a mirror so that I would be able to see my reflection. When I was nineteen or twenty, there was a girl I liked that would visit me at my place of work during the wee hours of the morning (I was a bellhop at a hotel, but for about a month I filled the night security spot whilst management looked for someone else to hire). I would take her into a dimly lit part of the hotel, and we would visit (there wasn't much I had to do between the hours of 10:00pm and midnight). She might have thought that I was taking us to a part of the hotel that was dark and had no one around (empty banquet hall) so that we could be by ourselves. Whilst that was true, and though it was nice sharing time with her, for me, it was nice mostly because I didn't have to worry about what my face looked like, as I had what I thought to be, embarrassingly-bad acne scarring. Sometimes when I would visit her at her apartment, when it seemed like we were getting even remotely physically close (her sitting close to me, lifting up my shirt and delicately touching my stomach), I would get up and playfully scoot to the other side of the room to offset my nervousness of being in a situation where either the slightest physicality or, even the remote possibility of sex (which I hadn't experienced, and she hadn't either) could occur. My bizarre standoffishness stemmed mostly from how bad I thought my acne scarring was (no one but myself ever seemed to notice). I remember, once, her taking me into the more-than-decently-lit bathroom of her apartment where she began rubbing lotion on my hands (it was the middle of winter), and me desperately wanting to get out of the bathroom for fear of what bright light would reveal. Eventually, I had five sessions of microdermabrasion (a hundred dollars a session). Though I felt a little better after my visits to the dermatology clinic, I had gotten to a place where I expected nothing from anyone anymore. What to say of one continually roaming the streets for the fairytale expressway but that they may be driven into the gutter of full disrepair. With feelings buried to the likes of that which would push one towards becoming a "walker of the earth," I began praying to God for a woman. A woman who would understand me, who would challenge me. When she came to me, I didn't want anything to do with her. I pushed her away, and yet she came after me with such a unique sort of strength that I eventually came to believe that my prayer had been answered. Let it be said that I was not the kind of person one wants to be dating. I remember calling her to come pick me up after having woken up on a street two cities away with a broken cigarette in my mouth at six o'clock in the morning. Even though she had to get up for school around that time, she came to fetch me with a graceful attitude. I remember on more than one occasion, phoning her to tell her that I would pick her up from work, and her having to walk home because I had passed out from drinking (sometimes I would wake up on my friend's couch to find that my pants hadn't informed me that they had had a piss party). I wet her parent's bed once, and when I woke and realized this, I snuck home without saying anything. My girlfriend, when she woke, called me and made me come back and take the bedding to the laundry. There were many pass-outs, many blackouts, and many an ill act done. What can I say but that I was a soul in need of correction, or more precisely, an alteration. What I needed was a spiritual tailor. And I needed someone in my life who understood that the seeds that I carried, as heated as they were, were buried in all but unfertile ground, keeping the untamed vine of my budding spirit from a most tremendous flowering. And she understood this. Let me tell you a story of a man and his train. Now this train, it roared through the land all but derailing at every turn, for it had been malfunctioning for quite a long time, and its operator, unable to redirect, saw his machine heading full speed toward the foothills of the Appalachian of isolation. The fire had plenty of coal. But the power of its engine was a pollution to many. Also, the cargo of this train did not seem to carry many riches. And one day, for some reason, when it passed a certain town, it broke down. And in this town, there lived a riveter. And when the riveter worked, she did so with the precision of a medieval clockmaker. And most of the town would come out to watch, for it was a sight to behold, for the fireworks of fastening and hammering were quite a show. But when the day was over, the riveter knew not the pleasure of another, that was, until the aforementioned train had broken down. Many of this town had heard of its operator, and of his unusual engineering, and the riveter too, and especially interested was she in his methods. And when he broke down, most of the town came out to gawk at him, but moreover, at his train: the steel and steam manifestation of a fantastic dream. The riveter offered to help this stranded man, and at first, he refused, but because the grit of her guts had shaped the correct bit of tenacity, he finally agreed, and thus did she that very instant, set out to repair and adjust, without modifying, that remarkably structured arrangement. And when the train operator looked to the town for aid that first night, most of its residents, like animals, were in want of something of the wealth of his carriage, but the riveter made way for this bemused and tired man to find comfort without a speck of hoggishness in her corralling manner of direction. The train operator watched the riveter work for days, and what he saw was more than great form, great style, for he had seen many with such. He saw something in the riveter that stood out like a dignified figure amidst beautiful, forgettable faces. Weeks went by, and in the downtime, the engineer and the riveter mingled. The train operator enjoyed the time they shared. He loved that even when the riveter was quiet, she was electric, a hum without a tune. The riveter was not the direct answer to the ways of the wayward, but to this poor stranded man, she was a great help, indeed instrumental in his admittance that he was never in his life comfortable with closeness, and that he only ever wanted to hole up with but those of an impartial bent. There was tremendous friction between the riveter and the train operator, but 'twas a conducive friction. That that produces a responsive development that can only arise out of the adhesion of collaboration in concert. By and by the engineer felt something he never did. It was as if death had grabbed ahold of the arm of his mortality to confirm the lethality of time. With the finishing of this massive effort, all but the strays of the town came together to honor such an event. And lo and behold, when the train was repaired, the smoke was a healthy billowing. As for the engineer and the riveter, well, they continued to work on what they together had built. After about a year of dating, my girlfriend and I moved in together near her college (her friend and roommate had graduated the previous year) so that she could afford to finish her last year of school without having to drive twenty-five minutes each way five days a week from her parent's house. When she graduated, I moved back home, and she did too. We broke up many times, only to get back together the next hour, or the next day. And one night, at some point in the six or seven months that we had been living back at our parent's, after one of our breakups, through the midnight hours, I wrote nine short poems, six of which, I still have. I was quite astonished by these nine poems that I'd written. I had never written a poem in my life, nor could I recall ever having thoroughly read one. And though the poems I wrote were simple, I truly felt that that was what I was supposed to be doing. The interesting thing was that it wasn't until I acted without regard to my future that I came to realize my vocation. Thus began my journey at the bottom of the world, wherefrom I climbed in blindness to illusions of greatness, surpassing my worth like a gnat soaring with the sense of a butterfly. It was around this time that I really started to read. I went to a library book sale and purchased my first two volumes of poetry: Reality Sandwiches and Leaves of Grass. These books were hugely influential for me: they were the first books that I had chosen to read for myself. These two poets (Walt Whitman and Allen Ginsberg) fevered my heart, kindled my soul, and brightened my mind. When I was an adolescent, I wanted to be a professional basketball player. When I was a young man, I wanted to be a filmmaker. And recently I've thought that if I wasn't a poet, I'd probably become a police detective or a radio personality. The police detective because I'm fascinated with that which it takes to solve crimes. And moreover, I'm fascinated by and admire the courage it takes to seek justice. Let it be said that the truest corruption is to be found in the corrupt efforts of any kind of police or public servant. O how wretched it is for a Lawman, whose job it is to protect you, to set out but to deceive you. The mind is an unlocked vault stashed with an intellect like a priceless artifact, but thankfully we can strengthen it to become capable of more than carrying out a well-devised con. The radio personality because I like the idea of sitting behind a microphone all day articulating challenging ideas, able to story-tell on the spot with millions at hand, taking calls and patiently listening to the questions and comments of interested listeners who, having dined on the spread of my tongue want a taste of the feast of my soul. This profession, or more aptly, vocation, appeals to me in kind of a born-mission way. Filmmaking is still quite a tempting desire of mine, and I think that if I were ever to make a movie it would probably come to light in both an unworldly and kitchen-sink-realistic way, beginning with a wide-angle shot of an unfathomably violent terrain like a mental lapse in the mind of God, fading to a wide-angle shot of a young man and woman in a desolate country backlit by the rising sun like the first explorers of the world or the last survivors of earth fading to a shot showing the sun slogging its way into the day illuminating the wretchedness of a major metropolis fading to a wide-angle shot of a dog limping through lonely alleys fading to a medium shot of other animals scurrying along or scrounging through the litter of the night's activities. There would be a medium shot of a disheveled woman in dancer's garb waking up on the street and trying to stand in a most careful manner cutting to a wide-angle shot of her falling into what seems to be a hush of sorrow. There would be a medium shot of a fire escape worn of its function like a broken xylophone and a close-up shot of a withering plant hanging out of its pot like the arms of an impoverished alien. There would be medium shots of middle-aged people with broken sandals eating at an all-night diner helmed by a waitress nearly as vacant as an entranced mystic. There would be a medium shot of a scraggly-looking man haphazardly dancing outside this diner cutting to a close-up shot of his furry tongue licking what's left of used sugar packets cutting to a medium shot of a woman sitting near a dumpster looking for cigarettes in her purse like looking for gold in a pantry. There would be a wide-angle shot of homeless people all huddled together in the free-range rest home of the streets like gnarled leftover meat waiting to be devoured by a savage god. There would be a close-up shot of an Ice Cream man with frosty glasses seemingly looking out at the world but with an expression as if the world wasn't there. There would be a crane shot of two men crossing each other's paths on the street cutting to medium shots of them shaking hands cutting to close-up shots of their faces seemingly looking as if for the first time they'd become aware of the lengths that may be reached through such a seemingly menial touch. There would be medium shots interspersed with close-ups of a man in an obvious stupor surrounded by walls painted with graffiti so bright that they seem aflame with an omen of hell or, merely ideas that shouldn't be received by a mind under heavy distress. There would be a lingering medium shot of a young, done-up woman sitting on the toilet in the bathroom of the diner, lifting her dress and piercing her thigh with a needle cutting to a close-up shot of her face noticing on the wall of the bathroom stall, passage after passage of peculiar comments that she begins to read aloud like a child repeating the words of the story her mother is reading her. There would be a close-up shot of a young man staring at a young woman out of the driver side window of a parked car with an expression that could be seen as wanting to sizzle or even fry in the heat of desire. There would be a medium shot of an old couple on a dimly lit street staring at each other as if each was looking for the look of love in the eyes of the other. There would be a close-up shot of a sickly woman staring out a window of a downtown hospital cutting to a point of view shot revealing her perception of the outdoor atmosphere as being uncommonly apt for a drastic conversion or, quite suitable for the stroll of a metaphysician cutting to a close-up of her face, clearly noting by her expression the psychological help she gets by her ascertainment of this. There would be a medium shot of an old man sitting in a well-worn armchair in a homey coffee shop, cutting to a medium shot of this man shakily standing before the roaring, mirror-shattered waters of a west coast ocean with a stare in his eyes like an animal looking for prey. There would be all kinds of shots at a higher film speed of a handful of beautiful youth like someone's impression of heaven cutting to multiple shots of them flaunting their bodies at parties cutting to a shot of a couple of them sulking in a half-drained bathtub. There would be many kinds of shots of the inside of a dive bar full of those who seem to have never taken a chance on the "good things in life": a medium shot of a young woman whose sway seems to make the promise of considerable promiscuity. A roving close-up shot of a distraught young woman swollen with drink haphazardly lying on a sofa. Wide-angle and close-up shots of a dingy diva singing a memorial-like ballad and, a medium shot of a young man sitting alone looking almost too shameful to speak. This movie would have voiceover narration by a faceless character. After the seven or eight months that my girlfriend and I had spent living back at our parent's, we decided to move into an apartment on top of a coffee shop. I was still drinking at this time, though not nearly as much as I had been. My girlfriend had gotten a job at the coffee shop that we lived above. And some months into her job there was a going-away party for her boss at a bar in town. I remember thinking that I could have just a couple drinks. Didn't happen. I barely remembered anything. I drove home, fell off the bed and blacked out. That was the last time I got drunk. The only time I drank after that was when my girlfriend and I were visiting my sister and her boyfriend (now husband) in Italy. I quit drinking entirely in my mid-twenties. And it wasn't until after I gave up alcohol that I truly began to contemplate the halt of my existence. I began to dig out of my soul that which I felt held the truth of the crisis of the world, finally reconciling with myself like the profound kinship that arises between those who had previously been the worst of enemies. The most difficult aspect of becoming sober was that I had to learn how to have fun again, and how not to let the blandness of my days drag like baggage through new passageways of enlightenment. Sobriety was, and is, for me, a profoundly difficult task. O to be able to shake off my grief like the foulest of rags! I had made a decision that could be referred to as taking the first step towards the beginning of a new world, yet the way I saw this world was the way a longstanding citizen of another country might view, with a particular romanticism, another land. I was no more familiar with myself than one is with, a country they've never visited. I knew that my soul held great riches, but my greatness remained a fleeting impression, as I was unaware of the process of its manifestation. Of all the blessings that sobriety allowed me, the ability to clearly think for myself, was, most certainly, of the most value. I had, at one point in time, written myself off (my incomprehension of school combined with my guidance counselor telling me that if I didn't go to college then I wouldn't make anything of myself, led me to believe that I was going to reach, in the future, the pinnacle of suffering, for I felt that I had been deemed worthy but for the purpose of slavery (a jailed body needn't have a jailed soul, but every jailed soul must live in the hell of a confined body). I thought that I was going to end up the most destitute of men. I saw myself in the post-school-scenario as but a weary, earth-roving wanderer, inevitably lead toward the barren landscape of the outskirts of the world, and that my flesh would be eaten away by eternal hunger). But as soon as I was done with alcohol, I began to think about how capable I was: I knew I was intelligent, but I also knew that my intelligence was a different kind of intelligence, as I was not conventionally smart, and I lacked, conversationally, all forms of academic leisure and articulate expression. I didn't have what society's educators would deem a traditionally respected, dignified intelligence. The expression of my intelligence via conversation seemed to be seen by the avid readers of the societal press as an incoherent mess: a sermon given by a preacher touting a lesser form of scripture. I knew I had a lot going on inside me (my yearning was such that it felt like a spiritual inflammation or an interior miracle waiting to happen), and that my mind was handicapped with an unprecedented aptitude for greater things, which could only have meant that I had genius. This view of myself quickly began to flood my mind to where I eventually came to a place (with the help of sobriety and the continuation of writing) that I was able to allow the greatness, backed up in my soul, to begin to truly take shape. Having struggled for identity through the lack of friction of such a floundering existence, when I finally came to, I felt extremely exuberant. It felt as though the dormant activity of my soul had become ignited with a fervor like that of a runaway fever. O how I wanted to firmly establish residence on the estate of my soul, for the soul is a magnificent maelstrom laden with spiritual activity, and I wanted to become lit down to my innermost crevice that I may partake in the utmost soul-shining endeavor. Prepared in my heart, aware of the debilitating psychological undertow, I proceeded ever so blindly into the vast, unlimited space of my inner world. O to come to one's soul like the first step of an astronaut upon an alien planet! With the seriousness of a great moral act, I began mining the depths of my heart to try and achieve familiarity with the furthest reaches of self. I began exploring my being but to find the most remarkable of unknown treasures. I've always had the fire in the chest, but I was now at a state where I could feel it spreading its meaning all about my being, leaving my mind with the strength of an irrevocable focus. The flame I carried began to spread to even the most dismal of passersby. I felt that the heat of my heart, unleashed, could produce an array of heavenly sights. I had reached a state in which I could not but see the future as but a most illuminated world. I felt as though something grand was investing in my soul. That I was being touted by some unknown messenger that I was applicable for the greatest of callings. I felt as though my soul had come under the surveillance of inconceivable powers. That I had possibly entered the divine framework seemingly having only to think to revamp the mindset of the world. I felt that I had somehow come to know something without knowing anything about it. This was the period of my life when I was at my most intense: I craved a reality that would match the intense yearning of my being. I felt that if I wasn't having visions then I wasn't experiencing actual reality. It wasn't long until I became fully enveloped in the notion that the soul is the sacred avenue through which every immortal thing enters the world. I came to think that my significance in connection to the universe was but a drop, as it were, in the cosmic pool, yet instinctually knowing that my soul may create a most roaring tide. I was ready to partake in the whiplashes of a mind mounted to a high rising dream (I had become a man who wanted nothing more than to fulfill his dreams, for dreams unfulfilled make memory but a place of tragedy). Through the reverent questioning of my belligerently passionate being, ever following a most peculiar thread of curiosity, many a night I solemnly stood in neon-reflected puddles, wrung out from the high-wire act of the heights of my mind. I carried visions of heaven in the world of my head, and, rather than growing the most repugnant wings of the earth, lifting but to rise to a most insignificant fall, I kept exploring without direction and with much turbulence, the map of my mind (feeling sometimes that I had become entangled in the strategies of uncharted galaxies), offering myself up to a most heavenly crash. I would find myself sailing my mind, all the while unable to find an island of consistent thought. My mind was like an endless plane of snow with infinity in every direction without a single track to behold. Sometimes thrushes of such immense beauty would bring about such a massive swelling of my heart like a kind of cosmic reservoir whereupon I would imagine myself sitting at the edge of the core of my soul like a mystical watering hole whereupon I would thus begin to fish the waters of the deepest abyss, reeling in a most radiant world and all its treasures therein. Many a day seemed to end without any tangible proof of my having had any special insight. But let it be said that there are experiences that cannot be spoken of. A music at work that one may never hear. I soon became fixated on the idea of a sober diner endeavor: meeting up with exhilarated people in a smoke-filled diner for an intellectual free-for-all. Ceaselessly teething on cigarettes and revved up with much caffeine I would, like a jack-in-the-box, spring forth with an out-of-nowhere excitement and startle those nearest me with a most passionate display of emotion. I would speak my words then intently listen to see if they had meant something. I found myself rising with a straight back out of uncomfortable chairs after long conversations looking for the next soup to break myself over as bread. Those who have nothing to say should tighten the gaps of their mouths like pinholes and sing a tune for those who are taking part in the dance. Never having been able to properly relieve my emotional tension, as I had only had a heart-to-heart with hearts as dense as stone (those souls burdening the air with their presence. Passing time but with pseudo bond-forming, side-dish communication, dragging their vacant gospels into the ear with the overconfident sound of a parrot. Those who love themselves no more than the insects they shoo. Those, secretly longing for what another seeks, who, when another finds such a treasure, show such a bitterly caustic tongue by rolling out a doctored accolade), I finally began to seek but those with the most impassioned hearts: those with solemn faces fixing each other's collars for the most extraordinary of meaningful experiences. Having met so many who've been ironed out of the frizziest originality, when I came in contact with a sincere heart, I would make sure to let them know I knew. The more I wanted to "live," the more I came to know how to get to know people. Many people perceived me inaccurately, but just as many saw me the way that I am, and thus showed me that I could rely on people as an aid to living, and thus allowed me to be more at peace on the terrain of the earth. With the promise of human connectivity swarming in my heart, many a day did I find myself sitting cross-legged in a stranger's kitchen. Having always wanted to become the walking display of the pinnacle of compassion, the best and simultaneously worst inclination of my sensitive being was to think that I could help people in the way that a Good Samaritan strives to be the greatest of humanitarians, for I felt that I knew with the utmost clarity the intricacies of the human heart. I felt that I, above most, could bring the most despairing of men to a great overflowing of joy. The idealistic and embellished way that I used to admire people like Patch Adams and Mother Theresa led me down a path in which I saw myself not just full of the utmost compassion (which wasn't true), but believing that if I fully gave myself, the pain and suffering of others would eternally dissipate. I've since matured (grown more reasonable). But that's not to say that I didn't feel or experience or reach, with another, what I would rightly call, ecstatic communion. Let it be said that we share, by way of the roots of humanity, the fruits of the inseparable vine. I think that there is such a thing as true connectivity, and that it may touch the most shattered of souls like a miraculous pollination in the most deadened of gardens. This period of my life (when we were living on top of the coffee shop) was when I became friends with those who live to be lit by the degree of friction that may bring about a miraculous fellowship of the soul in which one becomes eternally wedded to another. These new friends were an extraordinarily refreshing addition to my life, for I had spent most of my time with faceless men bowing but to those with handsome masks, and with others dire enough to remain unchanged, with boredom being the prevailing aspect of all their lives. And so, when I was involved in, or even on the cusp of real human interaction, the feeling within me could make a heart-rate monitor jump. I would try to gain all I could from real experience to eventually become fully shed of all falsity. Unless there's true reciprocation from one's soul to another, the grasp we claim to have of another merely consists of a mass of empty atoms, a vacant touch sheathed in familiarity. True connectivity is the constant purification of the soul, forever destroying the illnesses that may have been bred from the friction of dissimilar natures. I've always wanted, and will always want, a group of friends that will always be there for me to call upon: two or three people that I could go out with and have fun with and talk to and most importantly, confide in. But let it be said that having even one good friend feels like you're in stride with the upper echelon of humanity. That you're partaking in the essential experience envisioned by God for the life of men. As true gratefulness could never lead one on a path to eternal loneliness, does not a student of disregard become an advisor of alienation? I had become, over the year-and-a-half that we lived on top of the coffee shop, obsessed with the idea of correctness. I had become a complete perfectionist. I would wrestle out a line, love it, then ten seconds later think it was worthless. I've probably erased between five and ten thousand words. It wasn't until after my girlfriend and I moved to Portland, Oregon that I (ever so slowly) began to let go. Although it would take me almost two years before I would be able to actually complete a poem (beyond the first nine and a whole lot more that I've either lost or erased). To get to Portland with our belongings, we rented a car and took my girlfriend's as well. Her car overheated about three times, but eventually made it to town. We had taken a trip to Portland three weeks prior to moving there and spent a decent amount of our time on that trip looking for apartments. About a mile from where we were staying, we came upon an old, strange, gangly lady walking her dog. I asked her if she knew of any apartments for rent in the area, and she began to kind of speak about and vaguely point and drift towards the residence of a man she kind of knew that she thought might have something available. The apartment was a small, one-bedroom attic apartment in this man's house. The man renting the apartment seemed a little squeamish and paranoid, but nice. Whilst we were talking to him outside his house, he looked across the street, and then pointed to a particular spot, and proceeded to say, "The other day, right over there, I was having visions of the devil." We were slightly reluctant, but we decided to take this man up on his offer to let us rent this tiny, cozy, haphazard attic apartment. We must have really wanted to move or somehow thought that this man was to be trusted, because we had given someone we had met once, a three-hundred-dollar deposit, and furthermore, took his word that this apartment would be ours in two and a half weeks without having signed anything. We went home, let our places of work know that we were quitting, and then proceeded to move to the other side of the country. After having made our way to Oregon, we soon got jobs: my girlfriend, as a barista, and me, as a stocker. A year-and-a-half later I got a job working for Multnomah County Library. It was around this time that I was finally able to wash my hands of my preposterous perfectionism through thinking about the notion that, unwavering self-doubt cannot but cancel one's greatness out, eternally keeping one from perceiving the grandest portion of oneself, and also through my girlfriend simply saying, "sounds done to me," after listening to me read one of my not-sure-if-it's-done poems to her while she was making dinner. I finally felt that I had reached, or had attained, for lack of a better word, deliverance from the crippling effects of a kind of self-started drive towards depression and intellectual emaciation. This freeing up, this liberation, helped me to realize the strength of the illness of my previous state of mind, and thus helped me to begin to truly love myself (so much of my enjoyment of life seems to be dependent upon how good of an artist I am). I began to write, from that point on, without the notion of whether I was right or wrong, for what would one express constantly shackled to such moral deciphering? Having left behind that which I deemed trivial affairs, and, knowing that indecisiveness is but a constant incision in the swell of the heart, I wholly submitted myself to the highest task of the world: art: to, out of a most unruly water, render to the shore of the world but a most remarkable treasure. As difficult as the life of an artist is, and as distressed as I am, I don't ever want relief from this nearly insurmountable pressure, for it removes me from becoming the fall guy for the entrappers of the world. In a fascist regime, I could be charged with infinite counts of the crime of individual pursuit. I follow no path but move about like the route of an illegal taxicab. The intensity with which I write is like a wolf ravenously eating away at the flesh of the corpse but to find the juice of the heart. I work and scrape and dig until, in the depths of my soul, death begins to tremble, and a fluttering of life becomes apparent. I don't believe that even the best of what I produce should send the idea factory into bankruptcy, but sometimes I feel that the importance of what I have to say would keep the agendas of ignorance secretly hidden in the vault of unconscious memory. That the soul is subjected to things unknown, and is thereby, much fodder for a cosmic playground, sometimes, on a rare occasion of incredible intensity, feeling as though my senses were on the verge of becoming obsolete, and my heartbeat, the pulse of the world, I would slam my soul on the page with a might that I could barely muster. I would write with a frequency of heart unable to be grasped by the mind, and out of the most vital of these streams of words, I would try to execute what I hoped would be a profoundly resonating image. Afterward I would, in a mild reverie, rock back and forth in my chair whispering to imaginary crowds the words of my poetry, responding to imagined accolades by eloquently nodding and gesturing with a waving of my hands. At these times, when my mind would be agitated with such overabundant fodder,

I would step foot into the world (go out for a cigarette) and pace my apartment porch, feeling as though I'd long since been lost amongst the tribes of men. Sometimes I would feel as though I was a vagabond among the dead in a kingdom of shadows, and wishing that my every movement, my every gesture would become but the glorious spectacle of an ever-blossoming creation whereupon every one of my actions would become but the grandest of human moments. I was a virgin until I was thirty years old (I lost my virginity a little while after I got married). Growing up I was petrified of having a child. I couldn't fathom bringing a child into the world, mostly because I didn't want to disappoint my parents. I didn't want to have a child out of wedlock or, possibly be in the position of raising a child without a mother. And I didn't want to be in the position of having to stay with a girl just because we had had a baby. The other reason (a distant second) I didn't have sex for so long was that I was scared of not being any good at it. I didn't want to go through the devastating emotional experience of doing something so overwhelmingly intense only to go through the humiliation of getting reprimanded for "not being any good." I'd like to have kids, a few even, but I've always tended toward having them later than sooner. I don't think that raising a child at the present stage in my life would be devastating, but it would be reasonable to say that it might be quite debilitating to the life that I am presently leading, for I know that I would give all I could to the rearing of my child. I sometimes have an outlandishly idealistic view of how the raising of my children would be: I would like to live in a quiet, spacious, tree-canopied landscape. I would like the atmosphere to be filled with a most enjoyable setting for the grooming of the dreams of children. I would want to live in a place where real conversation is seen as an essential thing and where every soul sought to follow their dreams. I would want to see book-reading gatherings with the older kids telling their parents what book needs to be read because of the mood of the evening, the youngsters running or tagging, intermittently stopping to listen, their minds, awed by the stories, breaking down words that shall soon enough digest into a great swelling of their hearts. I would like to see, on Christmas, occurring in many a woeful soul a most delightful reckoning of the manor of despair. I would like to see the edginess of loneliness, ever alert, to fall asleep under the blanket of compassion. I would want to see the celebration of the fourth of July erupting in the streets into a most remarkable mixture of smoke and light to where at the utmost heights of this spectacular scene a miracle may be suddenly glimpsed. I would want to see preadolescents excitedly bobbling about like a training-wheel American walkabout. I would want to see, those, verging into adulthood, passionately exchanging the thoughts of their souls until what coalesces is but the profound comprehension of true connectedness. I would like to see the suicidal-minded oblivion-seekers, adrift from the sunken barge of the heart, arrive to the shore of the soul-mending consolation of a mother's care. I would like to know that a more-than-a-race runner has become strengthened by a newfound passion capable of taking him somewhere he previously thought was highly improbable. I would like to see provoked, by many a high-spirited adult walking by, a sense of wonder in all the children at hand. Likewise, I would like to see children provoke a sense of wonder in the deadest of grownup eyes. I would like the preacher of the local church to be one whose conviction and understanding of the Bible distinguishes him from double minded pastors and divides him from lukewarm Christians to where the minds and hearts of his congregation would never hear the Gospel in a laissez faire or perverted way, nor would the assemblage ever feel that they were but merely part of a religious reserves in an inconsequential spiritual war. I would like to see the good fathers begin to see their sons as more than that which is merely exemplary of good, well-bred offspring. I would like to see these fathers take the time to observe their young engulfed in the ultimate persuasion of the beauty of life (as all kids are), exploring the space of the world like a saint exploring the house of eternity. I would like to see the father/son relationship become a type of bond wherein what ensues is a remarkable understanding of the child's ability to foster the man within him apart from the father's doing. Likewise, I would want to see the same in the way of a mother daughter relationship and, also a father with his daughter and a mother with her son. I would like to see all parents regard their sons and daughters as truly their own people. For a child's life path should never be forced to begin with the road not taken by his parents. I merely would like to see something new arise within these parents, widening their perceptions like an alien serum injected into the stem of the brain. Lastly, I would like to live in an area where there is an abundance of children so that my children would always have someone to play with. I live a respectable life, yet 'tis a mere push from the void. I'm like the tightrope walker knowing more of the art as he continues to walk. I balance life as well as I can, and yet I know that if I were to fall, 'tis possible that I would become one whose life had become swallowed up in perpetual darkness whereupon I would become a frequenter of hellish establishments where strongly rooted grief has withered man after man, leaving one heaving and shaking, veering back and forth between the ranting of crackpot imaginings and that of the wretched display of subhuman disparity. Rather than accepting such a fate, I would hope that I would be able to at least eke my way into supplying myself with that which would keep me properly afoot for the maneuverings of life. Though deathbed memories might make my head veer to a most fantastical sphere, as the end might prove to be too conclusive a thing, I venture to say that I think the end will be beautiful because I will be able to see the pearls of achievement in lieu of my greatest perils. If I truly felt that I was not able to maintain a proper existence, I would probably take to the most out-of-the-way terrain, a rarely touched part of the map, striving but to find the place to which man has not yet gone, and thus has not yet had the chance to return, a place where such exposure cannot permit one to return unchanged. Though I would possibly end up destroying the temple of my body and the structure of my psyche with the most tempting of far-fetched adventuring, O the places within myself that would thus be apparent after such an excursion! As it is always so, such a risk may end up being the catalyst for a most catastrophic fall. One cannot weigh the pros and cons of such a venture without having already exited themselves from all they knew, for it may be too costly to reenter society. Having gained the willingness to be forgotten along the quest for answers, and as the fugitive is my spiritual brother, sometimes I feel like I've been exiled to a world far from the "kingdom of heavenly ways," leaving me wrestling with the effects of a most putrid atmosphere, as many a day I feel blasted with unmerciful winds, waves of the wickedness of hell. Sometimes the anxiety I experience I cannot help but think is as great as a bank robbery gone wrong. Many a morning I come upon a most despairing feeling, sending a massive tremor throughout my being rattling obscure the terrain of the world like an anxiety-ridden sun. My anxiety is caused, I think, mostly by how hard I work on my writing, for I have an exceptional need to accomplish great things before I die (I used to think that I would die at age thirty three), and though writing is such a difficult task (sometimes the task is so difficult that I repeat in my head: I long to be a minnow of thy spring and nothing more of anything), I'm at my most confident when I've recently finished a poem or a piece of writing that I'm fond of, for at those times 'tis easy for me to exist, for I'm brimming with the most spectacular mood of the ego, an impenetrable shield of self-worth. The other cause of my anxiety might stem from me feeling sexually inadequate, or from my loneliness, or from my emotional disconnectedness, for I don't know how best to please people. I'm not sure I know what their feelings are asking. Each soul is its own world, a planet with its own unique qualities, its own treasures. In its likenesses, it resembles the others, but in its differences, it couldn't be more dissimilar. Sometimes I feel that my being isn't inviting enough to permit many returns. Sometimes I'm conflicted about the extent to which I have to be aware of deceitful guests angling to partake in the hearty buffet of my soul. O how I yearn to glance the innermost truth of myself that I may reveal the bottom-level sameness of all men, from the heftiest of souls to those who've been deemed shameful oddities. Let it be said that one who cannot escape a "dog on a leash" relationship with one's parents, with learning, with friends, a spouse or religion, has no hope of ever becoming one capable of helping another properly grow and reap. The more I look back on my life, the more I realize that I was like the journeyman who loses his way only to find what another seldom finds. With that said, I've had to turn over many a new leaf, and am continually doing so. Moreover, I've had to stand up to that which seeks to endanger my soul. Though I'm capable of the trek through the deepest chambers of doubt, my life is a constant battle against the troops of unwanted memories. Some part of me thinks that the ideal life would be to spend all day in an endless greenhouse, taste-testing medicinal plants and, sit all night entranced in an opium den. I have, and will always have, a strong yearning to be closer with those that I'm closest with. Of those that I'm closest with, let me begin with my wife. This woman could give more life to the science of things by way of the blood being extracted from her back by the movement of invisible wings. She is, even in the worst of her sorrows, not without a capable flutter. I seek all that there is to be found in the soul of this woman: I yearn for the treasures of the sanctum of her soul like a geologist who longs to find the most sought-after of sacred minerals. Let us proceed to my sister. My sister is a great addition to our species. Her worries are, I think, reasonable for her kind of person. For she is constantly lamed by the violence of an uncaring world, and, spurred back to life with a rejuvenated spirit only through a rush of compassion for its inhabitants. I think 'tis her passion for life that keeps her "together," ever tightening the seams of her soul. My parents are people I've become, over time, quite disconnected from. But they are still a big part of my life. They are extremely giving people. They've provided me with that which helps me more than merely subsist in this pernicious precursor to eternity. And I have a few close friends of which we could aptly apply these words (in this strict formation): eye to eye—perfect proximity—anywhere. I spend a lot of time thinking about how much we don't care about others. About our extravagant lies. About evil agendas. But mostly I think about how much we don't care about ourselves. How much disease runs through the slab of the heart? How many of us live by an ideal concocted out of a misinterpretation of freedom? How many of us exist but like a suffocating man unable to die? How many of us feel held captive, or even ransacked of the tools of hope? If the most comfortable feeling is feeling comfortable inside oneself, then why does one consistently determine one's worth through the admiration of others? One need not fret over trying to portray oneself as an intelligent, worthwhile person, nor needlessly bother oneself with the question: how much of one is made up of ignorant mass, and how much a living, breathing, God-woven fabric. For having been made in the image of God, greatness comes to those who long to inspire, and be inspired. One of the most detrimental aspects of our society is that we fawn over well-bred horses without noticing the importance of the kick of the mule. As many of us are in constant practice of learning the dance of emotional stability, having a sturdy foundation is imperative in that it keeps one from adhering to unfounded principals, and thus keeps one from becoming constantly plagued by an emotional elephantiasis. Let it be said that happiness is all but a sham, 'tis joy that is trustworthy, as it seems to be given by God as a gift to unclog the soul to a fantastic rising of the spirit. Joy may be the most recognizable sign of one's passionflower in bloom. But remember: to recognize the song of oneself, one must know the melody to which the prophets added the words.

INTO THE FUTURE

I

Corporate empires challenge the
Sun for the territory of the sky.
Video-billboards shout advertisements
Like Pentecostal preachers.
Graffiti-plastered walls like hell with a fever of heaven.
Litter strewn about the streets like an ambitious perfectionist.
Regulated population zones
Like cousins of concentration camps.
Homeless shelters like yet-to-be-defined subcultures.
Impoverished school districts like the
Mindscape of a suicidal Grimm.
Unemployment offices like prisons with generous wardens.
Disturbing conditions of farms
Like a bible story told by a psychopath.
Military torture chambers splattered with blood
Like a hemorrhaging in the brain of God.
Prisons guarded by super soldiers with bloody feet.
Factories of a titan of industry like
Architectural manifestations of monstrous souls.

The atmosphere of many a street is such,
That, at any moment a crime could occur.

Dogs run the streets until
The darkest part of the night
Brings about the wolves.

II

A plentitude of shoppers hypnotized motionless
By the constant bombardment of pornographic
Commercials blaring from numerous,
Outlandishly-large city-street monitors.
PTA meetings buzzing with
Drug-induced nonsensical chatter.
Men in elegant robes one by one and by a
Trained footstep proceeding toward the center
Of the city square, each one leading by the arm
One of the select few that have been duped into
Being lobotomized for the debauchery of the wealthy.
A lavishly dressed man haphazardly naked in his car,
Strangling and bruising his penis whilst slovenly
Inhaling the "taboo pleasure" car air freshener.
Cockroaches infesting the homes of the impoverished
Like the field after the Super Bowl.
Ear-blistering dance clubs teeming with bodies
Swarming with untraceable sorrows that in the morning
Shall become strands of traceable diseases.
A few young men swarming with a darkening need
They think only forced sex could relieve, troll
The unsavory environment of dingy whorehouses
And damp cellars, looking to do much harm
In the stank dewy crevice of captive clit.
The proprietor of an urban porn shop egging on a
Group of wily teenagers like a carnival crowd
Anxiously waiting to see the latest freak show.
Under the glowing marquee of a downtown
Movie theater, a time-worn man hunched over
Masturbating like a snake shedding its skin,

Whispering trancelike atypical notions in the
Direction of braless bumpkin stumbling in the street.
Amidst the jarring bedazzlement of midtown
Advertisements, a blank-eyed Buddhist and
Oblivion-bound junky near a victim of arson in
Unequivocal agony rolling about in the streets
Like a biblical plague.
Nuns in the streets frantically looking for volunteers
To take a new kind of IQ test designed to show the
Difference between mere smarts and a visionary mind.
A petty thief looking—his being, as if having been pitched
Without the beams of reason—at the heartfelt glances
Of an elderly preacher at a roadside barbeque.
A friendship blossoming between a disgruntled mother
And a scraggly downtowner in a parking lot amidst
Piles of junk and the erratic sounds of the misfiring
Movement of a mechanical dime-store ride.
Professional Auto Racing has become
All but an extinct occupation because of the
Doing away with of "unsustainable professions."
A man with a hunchback putting forth his foot into
An upscale restaurant, facing the pivotal decision
Of which way to go like the
Old wooden sign at the fork in the road.
The expression on the face of a homeless man
On a busy street like an uncontrollable beast
In a petting zoo, and the manner of a man
A throw away from him like an amateur
Jester trying to impress the king.
A disabled man dragging like a seal in psychosis
Towards a blister-masked vagabond ankle-breaking
Towards an adolescent runaway trolling the
Streets with a mattress-toting drifter with a

Black-and-white belief in a Technicolor dream.
Behind the gate of the estate of a man whose
Personal property is like the goal of Edward Teach
Strut hormone-hulked guard dogs like mythical
Beasts glaring with malicious intent at a
Snarling crowd spitting the vilest venom.
A flesh-and-bone policeman saddled with
Cybernetic law enforcement like
A parody of online efficiency.
A chain gang of a thousand men strangling themselves
To death in the grotesque fashion of a provocative dance.
An elderly woman, agitated by backburner thoughts
Whilst trying to read amidst the nauseating light of her
Neighborhood laundry mat, turns her attention to one
Of the windows through which she sees a handful of
People lead by a man whose movements seem
Demonstrative of perpetual trauma, generously
Followed by the sluggish sway of a handful of bony teenagers
Entangled in obscene loyalty like human beasts of burden.
A middle-aged man unloading substantial grief
In the food court in a mall like he'd been
Wrung out to the sound of his innermost rattle.
An android-child at the dinner table with an
Expression on its face after being asked a
Thoughtful question like a planet
Knocked from its orbit.
Commercial carnival performers clowning around
With exhausted balloons whilst nearby an independent
Traveling circus working with a diligence like
Military men on the frontlines of war.
A street urchin trumpet's a sound that seems
To mourn the loss of "old world" ways.
A young woman with bruised arms and exotic eyes

Haphazardly sitting on a stool at the counter of a café,
Is reverently approached by a woman covered with
Interesting symbols like cultural pride or a character
Of a primitive epic, and shakes her hand with the
Faith of a wrist far beyond the belief of her fingers.
An elderly woman in her dimly lit den muses on
The thumbprint of a tearstained letter boldly
Plastered into the yellow dust of old paper.
A waitress reading passages on her break
Out of a book she'd been told
Fallen-down-persons should read.

Many are conceiving offspring in the hopes
That the symbol of innocence should
Shield them from harm.

An overweight redheaded woman with rouge
Smeared all over her cheeks like a mockery of
Raggedy Ann combing stretches of
Beach as vacant as the first days of creation.
A young man dreaming that the written word
Has become an indecipherable alphabet of
Interchangeable letters.
Oblivion by the pound on the
Nightstands of despairing professors.
Youngsters fingering their touchscreen devices
With the focus of expert codebreakers.
A wide-eyed, yellow-skinned cancer patient
Detachedly touched by a resident doctor as if
Being fingered by a stoic alien.
The look on the face of a babysitter at the sight
Of the behavior of a husband toward his wife like
A Capra character lost in a Scorsese picture.

Warehouses chockfull of that which shall be used
For the benefit of those who don't negotiate.
A young father standing naked under a bulbous,
Tumor-ridden tree begins raising
His chest under a hive of bees.
Self-driving cars turning here and stopping there:
Their inattentive passengers ripe for the rip and tear
Like the writing-off of damaged goods.
A young man sits in the darkest room of his
House, his face illuminated by the bulbs of
A dressing-room mirror, unflinchingly
Staring at his reflection whilst listening to the
Gleeful activity of the diner next door.
Young men slurping coffee and sucking down
Quarter-sized pills in a cozy diner, the meaning
Of their conversation as vaporous
As the argument of an atheist.
A woman sitting on her porch breastfeeding their
Newborn whilst her husband stares in her direction
As if he were married solely to a celestial affair.
The precise behavior of a middle-aged man
Sitting on the edge of his hotel room bed like
A poet on the cusp of something, or, one about to
Make of the downward spiral but an enchanting fall.
Two eighteen-year-old girls admiring their firm,
Scantily clad bodies in the living room mirror
Amidst the other partygoers absorbed in their
Technological gadgets like factory robots.
A group of young college men engaged in the
Age-old tradition of the panty raid as an excuse
To get to get to know a few girls without the
False aid of profile pin-up pictures.
Ambitious madams roving the dives looking

To recruit those of a most impeccable design
To be put to full use as the modern concubine.
A young man has turned his apartment into a
Plastic-covered haven for the spreading freely of
Semen, where, dark but for the three-dimensional
Image lavishly projected, he doggedly dances,
Placing himself inline with the movement of the
Phantom goddess, making sure his body doesn't
Protrude into that day's choice of illusionary
Flesh, thereby, shattering the effect of realness.

Mandated community gardens like
Manageable straightjackets.

A destitute man leaning over a vegetable stand,
Salvaging what he can of the slop
Like a landfill thoroughly gleaned.
A stream of headlights penetrating the
Darkness of an alley, revealing a man approaching
A group of pubescent boys absorbed in
Blood-brother activities, bearing a look on
His face as if he were about to
Settle a score with his soul.
The scream of a grown child-man as the
Light of his bedside lamp goes out
Like a purging of the soul of a superhero.
The presence of a pleasant tradesman working
In the large bedroom of a decrepit orphanage like
The overseer of the production of the universe.
A handful of wild-eyed men moving about
Under a busy overpass, quietly theatrical
In the flesh of their fallen foes.
An old woman in a woolen garment

Gathering little broken manmade things she
Finds in nature that remind her of the time she
Spent with her father when he worked as an
On-call repairman for an old clock factory that
Seemed to her when she was young like the place
Where God would go if he wanted to fix the world.
A clone questioning his creator the way a priest looks
To God for verification of his spiritual credentials.
Printed news is all but nonexistent except for
Secretly circulated pamphlets and hush-hush
Quarterlies devoted but to the bringing out of
That which lies in the shadows.
Undisclosed information uncovered
By a basement hacker like an archeologist
Having uncovered a substantial artifact.
A man lying in the middle of a busy street
With a large knife drooping from his neck
Like a piece or two missing from a jelly-filled cake.
A homeless man, sleeping on the sidewalk,
Rummaged through by a few scavenging
Teenagers—a blur of merciless faces—the scum in
Their hearts grimier than the foul mouth of their victim.
A man on a busy downtown street abruptly
Grabbing the nearest man's throat, feeling for
His trachea like a careless doctor, digging his
Nails into the man's tightened-up flesh, frantically
Gripping for the knotty cord and tearing out his
Tubing like the work of an impatient plumber.
The leader of a gang of seething psychotics in
Heavily frayed garb like a ravaged animal taunting
A young, drug-addled woman rattled by waves
Of grief into uncharted sufferings like a drummer
Battling for music amidst worn-out skins.

A man tightly bound in a mud-caked leather jacket
And a diamond-studded mask covering half of
His face, eerily creeping a vacant street in an
Impractical car with the radio blaring to a most
Threatening sound, ardently reaching for one
Of the multicolored contents spilling across the
Dashboard from the broken-strapped handbag, and
With a lipstick-smeared mouth and kamikaze-grin,
Spies a young woman in his rear view mirror
Moving across her porch in a fashion that could be
Construed as an inelegant brand of swooning or an
Unrefined romantic gesture, whereupon he begins
Shaking his body like Parkinson's and protruding
His tongue grotesquely imitating cunnilingus.
Amidst the eerie, distant sounds of viperous men
Mingling in disreputable dens and rusty wind chimes
Swinging from the porches of abandoned houses,
A mishandled youth like elegant fabric frayed
To the coarsest kind of material, struggling to
Maintain a sheepish demeanor after finding what
He found after waking up with a horrible hangover.
A man, speaking in a crowded auditorium with an
Ostentatious display of intelligence, and tears that
Seem to be manufactured for the podium.
A man with a frog-like composure sitting in a
Booth in a restaurant, intermittently glaring
In a straightforward manner at a man having
Blistered his soul in the furnace of havoc—a man
As frantic as an animal trapped in an ice rink—in the
Hopes of eliciting a response that prods him to speak
Seriously about his experiences in the hopes that he may
Rise from a catacomb of woes to a sustained reflection
On the possibility of true fellowship and interdependency.

A wealthy family gleefully abusing numerous children,
Losing themselves in perversions so great that the
Children's memories are too scathed to be filed away.
Amidst the chic décor of a high-class brothel, a massive,
Handicapped man like the wreckage of a well-built ship
Trying to cool himself with a broken fan whilst struggling
For breath like an allergenic plague, reluctantly accepting yet
Interiorly relishing the indifferent acceptance of a prostitute.
The perverted shenanigans of a secret gathering
Taking place in a suburban setting like Norman
Rockwell having gone down the rabbit hole.
A man ousted from civilization, consumed
By a disparity exhausted of the sporadic pleasantries
Of grief, finds himself
Trolling the briniest tunnels in the most desolate section
Of the city, whereupon he is approached by a man
Of unquestionable presence (a ferocious inquirer, a man
Whose whistle-blowing morals have rendered him a
Kind of chaplain of the streets, a man hastening to places
None seem to have lighted, and, seemingly have not
Bothered to seek), seeking but those with gasoline dreams
Awaiting the spark of the friction of thought.
Amidst the barbarous screaming of overzealous
Spectators in the stands of an underground arena
Scattered with disorderly mounds of unclothed people,
A loosely robed politician in a barbaric stupor of pleasure
Like a Roman emperor, periodically pausing, not knowing
What to lose himself in like a demented warlord surveying
His captives . . . eventually obeying the notion that his
Life may be worth something if he masters them—turns
Them as hopeless as the abyss is deep—damages their
Spirits like the wings of child-captive insects.
Transhumanists expunging themselves from the pool

Of humanity like smudges on the pages of the
Lambs Book of Life.

A man of triumphant beginnings, of a slippery middle,
And of recent decline, a man who has long since
Decided to labor to discover the truth of himself—
To bowl over but that which cannot be eradicated
From the soul like the dust on the framework of Adam,
A man whose tormenting endeavors have led
Him to become the unofficial dean of a school
Of thought adopted by the maddeningly troubled
Navigating the labyrinthine lie of the world—
Shepherd's those ever in search of others of the
Like in the hopes of spawning an underground
Network inclined to survive what has been
Prophesied, and what had been pushed as
Far out of the mind as could be pushed.

Many a wall guarding from wind and witnesses.

Subway tunnels are helpful hollows.

III

This is a world of hardship, of grief, of loss.
This is a world created by those without the ability
To understand the implications of their creations, for
Technology is a form of advancement whose
Final achievements remain unknown to man.
And the tidal wave of this advancement
May leave the palace of the soul in ruins.

The dragon of technology has risen in direct
Opposition to the knight of reason with but the
Mission of covering up the tracks of humanity.

Technology is a helpful thing until its advancements
Become the barometer for our well-being.

We have placed our lives in the hands of corporations
And government operations which, aided by the
Bombardment of the sham of progress, has bore
Within us a great disease, and has thus staked its
Claim as a predominate force in our lives.

Who are the caretakers of the world?
In whom does truth reside?

Idolatry has never been more alluring.
We worship what we think gives us a better life,
Even if the natural in us is no longer able to thrive.
We decorate ourselves with beautiful wreaths
But constrict ourselves with unnatural work.

What would man become if he should lose
The sensory-wisdom of tactility?

Bleak in vision and purposeless we drift, entranced by
Ingenious gadgets and the deception of advancement,
Ever blinded by the mindsets we are
Given to think with.

And though the heart is a hydrant through which
The mind may be cleansed, until one leaves false
Pursuits behind, he shall be left but with the

Growth of the hellish squirms of the soul.

The spiritual drought of man has left the forces
Of hell full reign to roam the darkness of being.

As many a man woman and child are being
Black-market born by a rational doctor,
Leaving what will be of the inextinguishable blueprint
Of divinely printed putty, the lives of the majority
(Through an emphatic acceptance of genetic
Modification) continue to be born without the
Holy anointment of God, whereby even the most
Determinate of men may become the most
Efficient of slaves: life must begin as an unaltered
Species lest inequality become an inescapable fact.

This is a world in which freedom has
Become more important than refuge.

The confining route of cyberspace has restricted
The mind to a limited amount of answers, deterring
One from want of questions, whereby the breeding
Of original ideas rarely transpires.

We must see the mind for what it is: an uncommon
Expansion, the Sahara but a footprint
In the trenches of its vision.

For the mind is capable of taking full reign
Over the body like the sun over new territory,
Shedding light upon every facet of thy being
Like the reopening of a factory.

One is no longer queasy at the thought of their
Intellectual friends asking their dads tough questions,
And yet they should be frightened that such questions
Are no longer being asked.

Through all but the sterilization of one's mind
And heart, we've come to see quite a debilitating
Erosion of the infrastructure of the psyche
Whereby the sky of the mind no longer seems
To be capable of the hue of a most radiant clarity.
No more do we marvel at what we can't quite fathom.
We've become a species that, because of our
Susceptibility to distraction and quick knowledge,
Scarcely ventures to discover, and yet we purport
To be well-fed with wisdom, and,
Well balanced with meaningful strides.
We purport to understand the way in which
We can develop, but we don't
Understand what it is to *truly* develop.
For the majority of us are caught up in an
Abundantly populated yet obscenely fabricated
Social life, like the continual planning
Of a party that will never materialize.
We look without saluting, greet without touching:
A world of unsuitable suitors engaged
To fantastical lovers.
We've become as unfamiliar with one another
As the most distant of planets.

Indiscriminate flattery cannot keep
One afloat in this drowning world.

Heavy debates and healthy quarrels are all but

Nonexistent, for this is a world where no one
Cares enough to object to another.
And this is a world in which lust is praised:
Pornographic advertisements featuring overly
Gregarious bodies ever in search of a new hide to ride:
The young know what it is to lay before they can read.
And though a traditional body (all parts human) is still
The most sought-after commodity, an artificial
Substitute is in high demand, especially for those
Who've long since given up on the risky affair
Of the human-flesh-endeavor (those who squirm at
The thought of the debilitating shame
Of not being able to please another).
Can one maintain a reasonable way of life through the
Bogged down existence of such a detached society?

We move throughout our lives like Pinocchio with a
Blue-Fairy-attachment but without a Geppetto foundation.

We are advancing, yet our spirit is lagging.
Sickness is much more sickening.
Emotionally we are weakening.
Psychologically we are breaking.
Marred in the mind, scarred in the
Heart, and ill-footed as we are, we are
More than merely a flawed people—
We are a contemptible species.
And because of such horrendous indiscretions,
The soul seems but an irremovable stain.
Freedom for the free is a pursuit gone astray,
But for the captive, 'tis a hell all but
On par with Christian reckoning.
Modern slavery is the business of evil on a mass scale.

The numbers are as big as a tycoon's will.
Despairing as a free man may be,
Comparatively his song is a heavenly tune.
And as some of us are merely waiting for the
Day to give way for the easy maneuverability
Of the camouflaging of the night, some of us are
Sold into slavery, and thus are sold, in many cases,
By those and to those with bestial norms, to those
Whose seeming power deems all else naught.
Our vulnerability is taken advantage of by
Monsters whose tongue-tied evil is expressed in
Gestures of elaborate grisliness, and whose brail
Of depravity would comatose the blind.
Some of us are forced to experience a darkness
Normally reserved for the ceremonies of the savage.
Some of us are forced to be ravaged by
Sex-buyers salivating like animals after the kill,
And thus, are forced to bear the frays and maims
Of the lining of thy soul by those whose natures seem
To have been determined but by the scars of the heart.

How dark is the heart?
And have we only seen but the
Froth of its wickedness?

If the world were mere fantasy,
How much of it would be overrun
With trolls, ogres, and the like?

Man, because of his sin, has thus
Walked the plank into
The darkest waters of being.

This is a world in which one is unable to
Keep oneself from crossing a certain threshold
Whereupon one catches in the trenches of the soul
The vilest sediment at the bottom of the world:
Ill Messages spread like debris in the wind, dropping
The seeds of false commandments into the very
Grain of our being, greatly contributing to our
Incapability to cope with such a drastic climate.

The powers of the mind must coincide with the
Virtues of the heart, but having split the wood of
Ourselves with inborn vices, where should
The timber hold, what rot shall enter its crevices?

Along with taking care of one's body, one must
Also keep clean, the cracks of his being, lest
The soul become but a host of poisonous activity,
Spreading disease throughout the world.

Unable to evacuate or properly cultivate,
All we see is dismay and hardship.
This is our lot, and we accept it.
Yet our blood is running, and we are manic.
Thus, we are more than distraught like
Butterflies broken by the wind.
One must win a daily battle within oneself
In order to proclaim oneself sound.

Memory is the oil in which the bread of identity cooks;
And though we can't remember what it was that first
Began to ail us, as haunted by the "memory-ghosts"
Of the psyche as many are, many still hunt for real
Recollection, whilst others seem to give up their lives

To merely play with the toys of another's dream.

We've become lost on the path to the kingdom of being.
Purposeful strides have become all but an inept step.
Stray animals walk the way we wish we could lead.

Many a man, having previously been able to grasp enough
To be able to make some sense of living—having with
Battleship-character made their way through glaciers of
Mounting hardships—is no longer able to walk with
A most dutiful poise, and thus may be eaten by emptiness
Until he is but a chaos of unsubstantiated stuff.

Some think, were there a cure for despair, it might
Be found in the tapestry of connectivity tightly woven
Between those of similar natures, those who
May remain ever radiant through the
Emotional fraying of such delicate fabric.

Many are craving authentic human connection,
Their moral compasses still northerly swaying.
But goodwill towards man no longer
Seems to be a reasonable notion.
We must break our conventional practices,
Confront our cyclical ways.
But we're unnerved by the person we're always with.
Aghast at our own intellectual properties.
Petrified by the stuff we don't bring forth.

Because the soul is eternal, hope is therefore
Contingent upon the full breadth of thy spirit.
Thus a burden improperly weighed
May become a landslide of grief.

We must remember that we're accountable people
With feelings tangled up in our core
Like the ropes of the sail after a storm.

One's health fades, and possibly, so does one's will.
What doesn't fade is the eternal nagging of the soul
Like the spiritual remnant of an aborted baby.

We've become complacent—
Take no initiative to
Relinquish ourselves from reliance.
We bow to the wants of others.
Are caught in the vortex of desires.
Lose ourselves in fantasies.
Adhere to the illusions of
Prodigious stature and ambitious deeds.

Those whose grain runs counter to the slickness
Of worldly acceptance are deemed ignorant
And reckless; and since crucial responsibility
Recruits us on a daily basis, many therefore
Escape themselves with temporal pursuits.

All illness begins with self-avoidance.
And if one continually sidesteps the self,
One shall end up whoring out his integrity
For approval and validation of worth,
And, for, the nominal pleasantries of praise
And commendation, leading one to
Give up his life to feed on sustainable straw
At the trough of another man's dreams.
And the tragedy is that 'tis a mutilation

Far beyond a surgical one.

Let it be said that purpose isn't something looked for.
Every soul that has ever added breath to this planet, is,
Without question, created with massive,
Innate significance.
A most remarkable story, if told.
But to be told, it must be lived by
One known by another.

Are the stories of the lives untold,
Played out in the dreams of God?

IV

No more are our lives filled with red-letter days.
The illusion has crumbled.
Reality cannot be masked,
Like bone escaped of flesh.
So dire is our circumstance that
Many a soul lacks in tenderness
Like a shade of Cain-color red.
Many have lost life in their eyes
Like owls wide awake in the day.
Many please themselves until the
Desire for pleasure makes them
Rave without order or manner.
Many are secretly battling their cries
Whilst indiscreetly seeking play.
Many suffer more than the pangs
Of loneliness when close enough
To someone for the possibility
Of a conversation to arise.

Many walk in gestures they hope
Should keep one from gesturing them.
Many think it not worth it to step foot
Back on the property of society unless
Every drop of shining sea and crust of land
No longer presents the possibility of freedom.
Many have hidden their hearts away
Like veteran hoarders.
Many hide from the truth of themselves
Like caterpillars unable to molt.
Many mask their shame in a most
Bombastic manner by taking up the
Illicit crusade of the loins, committing
Barbaric acts driven solely by the
Fever of the sickness of coveting.

V

The necessity for proper human development
Is imperative, but because of the unconstitutional
Activities of the government, the rampages of
Tyranny; because of the lack of parental guidance,
And the manipulation of education; because of the
Lack of intellectual prowess and imagination;
Because of our apathy; because of the bankruptcy
Of the interior economy; because the broth of the
Intellect lacks the sustenance of a proper meat;
Because many have left behind the train of reason
From what they thought to be the placid platform
Of life; because of our adherence to illogical theories
Peddled by untruthful or misguided practitioners;
Because of hateful ideologies, false beliefs, and
The worship of false gods; because of the impulses

Of wickedness that we've come to regard as but
Peculiar jolts of un-had freedoms; because of living
Too long in doubt, flailing in fear too often; because
Of working without risking, and learning without delving;
Because of the lies we've mistook for lives;
And because of our fear of drawing a line between
Right and wrong, we've thereby become a people
In need of an intellectual resuscitation.
But more importantly, we're in need of
The great safehold of the mercy of Christ.
For unless one forswears all self-regarded adeptness
And gives himself over to the Lord, he won't be able
To live without begging for life from the world.

For if any be born anew in Christ,
He thereby becomes His true child,
And thus, he will be given the strength and
The power to let every lashing he
Takes, strengthen his will.

There exists the sort of love that was, is,
And will always be.
And grounded in this love was the
Federal head of the human race,
The righteous under the Law of Moses,
and those whose foreskins of
The heart have been taken away.
Thus has this love been shown to man from
Time immemorial, and shall continue
To be onward through the gates of eternity.
Therefore, let it be said that one has a
Brother in the backrooms of the just, in the
Cellars of the righteous, in the trenches of

The godly, and in the caves of the saved,
And thus, in the hearts of believers,
Where man not only has allies, but
Where the roar of his grief is embraced
More than a philosophical mouthpiece.

The Fall runs far beyond the plane
Of dust and water, and deeper still.
For born in sin we are, and, imprint our
Pride we do with the corruption of our own understanding,
And stamp our own perversion of the truth.

VI

Whether you've become all but
Deaf to the knock of life in thy pulse; whether
Thy misfortunes feel like the maximum penalty
Of your misdeeds; whether ye feel that ye are
Unable to regain thy footing as if thy footsteps
Were bound to oblivion; whether thy anxiety
Makes ye quake like jostled membranes; whether thy
Sorrow has kept ye from acquainting thyself
With another; whether ye live in the wilderness
Of a traumatized mind; whether ye have
Committed unimaginable indiscretions; whether
Thy life has been a constant escape from a world
In which ye must constantly fight against becoming
Yet just another soul manipulated or controlled;
Whether ye have taken it upon thyself to try and
Relinquish thyself from all thy baggage, from all
Thy worries, and from all thy anguish by having
Begun to make decisions based solely on ethical reasons;
Whether ye feel confident that ye have found

The reasons for the issues plaguing thy soul; whether
Ye profess to know thyself to the bone, and thus
Have charged thyself with but the task of utilizing
Thy gifts; whether ye have stood before another
Without showing any symptoms of the illness
Of bone-stricken indifference; whether ye
Are hunched with burdens; whether ye feel
Interiorly like that which must be similar to the
Feelings a fisherman has after having successfully
Charted the part of the sea that holds the most delectable
Of delights; whether ye believe that the further ye
Are from the world, the closer ye are to the truth;
Whether ye feel like ye have achieved a most
Rapturous state; whether ye feel like you've
Gained the most sought-after role in the most
Spellbinding of plays; or whether ye believe
You've made strides few could surpass . . .

Unless ye have forsaken thine own will by
Letting go of the faulty stronghold of pride,
Ye shall continue in bondage to sin,
Continue to suffer at the hands of
The most prideful sinner who
Corrupted his wisdom for the sake
Of his splendor, and thus became
A fuming fury void of light.

Unless ye forsake thine own will, ye
Shall continue to be plagued by the ills of
Deception, and thus shall be unable to
Discern the chaos of evil rampant
In the darkness of thy soul.

Do you not feel, in the depths of your being,
The murmur of a prayer which you do not concede?
Is desperation not the last order of grief?
Alas, do you not feel gridlocked in spirit?

Let it be said that repentance is the foyer
From which one enters through the door of Christ
And comes into the perfect garrison of grace.

And if one should be given the power to
Believe, he shall thus be strengthened by
God like the marrow in the bones of Christ.

THE WALK

W E WALKED AMIDST THE desolate terrain; our bodies not bruised as much as our hearts were blistered. Grief-laden we dragged along the parchedness under the blinding presence of the sun, its brightness seemed bright enough to block out darkness; but soon enough it began and moreover lingered, which made easy-breathing air feel choked like a fool in a group of wisemen. And we all took note of this, and just kept on. And we felt unwell not knowing but kept walking but felt like crawling. And it was not long until we entered what seemed to us a most sorrowful and ruined town where we thought a blameless man might be hard to find. And not long after this thread was sewn, a man nearby that seemed wooly-thick in thought told us how petrified of the more-than-tick-deep sins pervading the underneath skin he was. And then he pleaded with us to run along beside us, and then, with frantic curtness, told us of a dream he had the day before: "From the thrushes of blackness thrashing against the windows of my soul, and the temptation of alarming desires, with a most vehement surge I shuffled forward like one from a wreck whereupon I scanned the land to see where I should persist, whereupon I felt that I was at the whim of whatever was at hand, whereupon a profound fear awoke in my heart, whereupon the divine harmony of the horizon became a most ferocious tone, whereupon all forms of life began to vanish and what arose was a most woebegone landscape, whereupon for some reason I went staggering towards the most wayward of these plains, whereupon I began to see amidst a firmament of burning skies an array of sights more horrifying than that Noah saw in his dreams, whereupon I found myself in a land that seemed the bottommost level of the world whereupon I saw a-ways off traveling people, and with that I came to." "And because of the realness of the dream, I went out to see if they were not there outside but only dust and animals; and then the neighbors came and laughed and spat on me and called me witless—said my way got in the way of me and spat at me again like a whore woman. They had never liked me much because I could not fend for my own eating, for I was never good at farming. I was people interested much more than anything, because when I watched them, I thought about things you cannot see that made them do the things they did; and, also why they made them do these things. But they hated me and called me gutless. The only people that allowed me near them was a family who did not scold me really; but I think they saw me close to swine. But still it was good being near them, and I think they sometimes did not that much seem to mind. And I loved to be there when one of their children was allowed to play outside, because that meant that I could watch the child do what favorite things they do outside. And once I watched the youngest girl speaking to herself in the dirt; and sometimes when there was a bird's nest nearby with baby birds in it, she would go get two little sticks and make them dance all along the branches nearest the nest, pretending that the sticks were a part of the bird's family. And sometimes I would tell her mother that I had often watched her son and oldest daughter; and sometimes would watch her youngest one for almost an hour; and that I saw her children as those who would push through what people must push through, and that I thought they would push as far as people can go; and the mother sometimes laughed and told me to go back to the slop and do like the lower do, but sometimes she would be real quiet and look at me with a grin that hurt her the longer it lasted. I never knew when I should ever go around her or her kids. But I sometimes snuck memory pictures of the oldest daughter, because I loved watching her play when she thinks there is going to be a storm, because she whispers to all the plants she can find, to let them know not to be frightened of what is coming, but they seemed not to listen to her, but only to the nervous breath of the howling wind. And sometimes she would ask her brother to join in when she would make a play-story; and when he would ask her what it was going to be about, she would tell him she never knew until a little while after she started, but that he should just start walking, and if she thought he was playing, then she would tell him things to do and then hopefully the playing would start to become something she could make something more of. And I would watch the man helper too. His way was like a storm in fair weather. His behavior was such that he would sometimes latch onto an idea or some such thing that seemed to consume him, and he would take off his shirt and start fidgeting with wood and the like. And after a while of this kind of doing he would walk quietly to the edge of the wood and perch his half-naked body (profusely sweating in the bright glare of the morning) on a large, jagged rock. I liked to watch him very much, the man helper during these times, because I knew he was showing you without knowing he was, some of how he was; and I thought the way this man wandered and spent his time signified an urge for something. But let me tell you one more thing about the mother: she made me nervous. I never saw someone more in herself—and sometimes like an unopenable chest. And sometimes when she was not tending to the children, she locked herself up in her room doing I cannot recall what. And sometimes she would roam through her house like an empress surveying the charms of her palace. And when she was peculiar and moody, sometimes her body would tense, and her behavior would become wholly different. For sorrow frightened her because it made her feel like death was chaperoning the day, and that its progression of enveloping her made her soul available somewhere. And at other times she felt comforted by it, because she said she knew God worked in the shadows. And so, when I had this dream, I went to her, and she shooed me off, but before I left, she caught me by the wall of stone and said, "If ye find these people and therefore know the dream is true, come fetch me and I will join ye like quilted leather." "And so, when I saw you all I knew how real it was, for I felt it in every crevice of my existence, especially in the uttermost cracks of me. I so wanted to tell you all of what was shown to me, and ask you who maybe brought it there, but first, the mother, may she come with her oldest? Say what you will, and I will obey." And the head of us said, "Come, and them too if they seek to forgo their homestead for rough-road strain and dreadful worry, for the off-trail ways are without direction. If thy word is whole-heart true, then firm footed we will stay a while, but go get the woman fast or kill the ground we will with too much waiting." "And so came along I did, and the mother too with her oldest. Her man-helper and daughters stayed to reign over the lasts of life at home." Away didst go our tribe, and that night we roasted our tender matters in the communal fire, and our questions baked until their whys were answer-served. Most of us seemed answer-filled, but the mother figure who was tied with caution like a caught animal, went to sleep that night like a first-day prisoner. At the cockcrow, the mother figure, with ankle-anxious steps followed us into the drowsy day. And when the sun had woken all the way, we came upon a letter nailed to a tree that said, "For you who have come this way have I left my testimony that ye may know from what blindness came I from, and because of what have I come to see. The bud has barely bloomed since Jesus of Nazareth, the one called Christ has died and risen. I did not sing His name, nor did I know myself any trivial things of Him. For I was a lowly sort and cowered under hearsay. On the day I looked upon that burdened tree with hopeful eyes, like stubble from fire went my fear, and before His flesh began to turn, I knew the Lord. I scribe thee this that ye may know the course I take cannot keep death away, but air-breathed life cannot repay the cost to keep its course." After we pondered, for many minutes, this confession, the head of us lead us onward, and it was not long until we came upon a woman in sheer delight; upon her neck, tough scars played their bounded slither. We waited till her joyous tussle slowed before approaching. She took note of us with wild eyes, and before us slowly paced. And then the head of us greeted her with mild gestures, and away she went with what we wanted. And the head of us asked her what place she had in such wilderness as this, and she said her life is not in the hands of this dusty expanse. And at that, our fellow traveler questioned her more, and on she went, saying, "Hated as I was, and mistook for one accursed, escaped I did. And if I were to get caught by the guardsmen, or dreadfully by the king himself, the chances of escaping punishment would be as good as coming across a well-mannered goat; not but a forsaken desert did I claim for walking ground, and lake water for quenching thirst. I took for dwelling an abandoned cave. And on the night I ate the meat, the life of which with mine own hands I took, I took to asking with my heart who assigned my lot; and some time into the night I looked toward the cooking flame and saw a man of nowhere fingering the sand into no such pictures of frilly finery, but scribbled words like a mating harvest, and I quickly inched forward whereupon came I to notice what he wrote. And when I turned my eyes from what was written, I shook like a wind-tossed leaf." The woman then bowed her head, and said, "Since then I have never left this my dwelling place, nor cared how I am cared for, for cared for will I be." And at that, we departed and came upon the southern sea, and saw in the distance a woman gathering reed, and at the sight of us she waived us come. And as we neared, she eyed the second youngest of us, and depart from us the child did, and rested herself within this woman's frame, whereupon the woman handed her a half-woven basket and said, "Labor on that which the maker has laid upon ye to do." And as the child went to work on that woven imperfection, all took rest but the mother of us, for she bathed the one of us who by herself could not. And soon after we woke, we journeyed on, and when the midday sky took to comfort a tired sun, we saw a man not too far who seemed unconcerned with what lay about him. When we came upon him, we saw that he was wounded, and when he noticed us, he turned his head like a reverie and went on about how the wickedness of man is sheathed in gilded glory, how pain is covered much with pleasure, and how ungodly men of lofty rank are bound to miseries beyond the sorrows of battle. And he went on about how when time began, the mists of sorrow over-borrowed from its dreary banks. And then the man turned away, and at that the mother of us coated him well with wares, and then eyed the head of us and went yonder into the bush to ponder. And when she returned, we journeyed on and came upon an inn, a dusty mote. The keeper mumbled toward us wearing on his feet slippers tipped with beaks of birds that scratched the floor as he motioned for what we wanted. And when the head of us stepped forward with his questions, the innkeeper pointed with outstretched arm towards the part of the land with decaying trees and then went away like an untrained dog. And we thanked him and quickly left. When we arrived to where the innkeeper pointed us to, the seer was waiting in her place of rest: a room with soft bedding and pictures in place of windows—candles lit the darkness. When the seer saw us, she tilted her head and nodded come, and this we did. But both our mother figure and the head of us did reluctantly. But we went, all of us, and gathered round her, and said why we had come. And when she waived us down around her, the head of us began to ask about the pervading feeling of evil and death and what of Jesus, and the diviner sat halfway up and with a prepared directness said, "He was a heretic to many." And she also said not to say that name around these parts. And the head of us asked, "Why, is he a threat?" And the soothsayer said, "There are some who see him another way; even I see him as a dangerous sort, for I haze when I gaze in that direction." And a few of us began to sit, and the seer said that the mother of us must go away, lest there be interference. "I do not dare realize for that woman." And we all took such significance from that and began to file out when we were told we could stay one and all, and we did except our mother figure, who but listened at the door. After a little while our mother figure closed her eyes and began to speak, moreover pray out loud, "Jesus of Nazareth, if you are the Christ, fill this room with truth and holy doings; let us not be deceived." When the mother figure prayed, the tongue of the astrologer driveled notes of a hideous tone whereupon we stood numb and breathless, and then out we hurried one and all questioning the mother of us as we went about what knotted thoughts made her unravel-speak such a string of words, and she thus replied, "I said what was laid upon me to say, for I was fearful, and the wisdom of mine own comprehension seems a gnarled root of lies stemming tendrils of deceit writhing within the clays of the muck of my soul, and so, before I prayed aloud thinking I was of the letter nailed upon that tree. I asked God to give me the wisdom of discernment to exercise me after the seer spoke." Away with her son the mother figure went, and off we followed. Soon enough, burden-dark the light became, and we captured enough wood to light our space of darkness. We gathered round the starting fire and spoke with solemn tone of hopes unknown, and all the while did death seem to our territory bound. That night, while the talk did still yet abound, one of us asked our mother figure what would come of what we sew, and the mother of us said, "I do not know, but a harvest of truth we are sure to reap." And with that, silence fell too harsh. And when morning loomed, it seemed a dreadful glow, but on we strode and entered a town where children played and played, and dust from the earth went up like an apocalypse to the ants. After the dust began to settle, we turned and saw a man standing quietly serious in front of the well. After the head of us filled our pale, this man, now not a pace away, not halfway clothed and no longer parched when he knew we were composed with him, went and freed his tongue with greetings, and at that the mother of us waived him toward our camp. And while he ate, the way she looked at him told him more than what she could say. Too much were the feelings inside him to reply with a nourished gesture, and so the mother of us fed him more bread and meat. The rest of us gathered round; and after his ravenous display, the head of us began asking this man wherefrom he came and what his course, and at that, the disheveled man told us of the time when he was a boy and he came to know the truth of his mother: that she practiced things that were not for the wellness of children nor good for the minds of adults. And he told us about her learning necromancy, and about how the community knew of such dabbling but did not rebuke her, for they sought her tells and were in want of her secret learnedness: her conjuring and wizardry. "When my maturity came, I left home in want of truth, which has brought me to many towns and people. But not until the year before the last did I cross the border of all falsity and come to know the truth. For one night when I was, after supper, drunk in open wilderness, looking over the vastness of the earth, I saw, walking on a lake of black water, angels mourning gasping and heaving with sacks of tears bloated beneath their eyes; and when this vision faded, descriptions were unavailable to me, but I knew things most need sense for." And at that, our fellow traveler hastily questioned him of this truth he bannered, and the man said, "Above all, are ye sinners, and if ye but tout thyself, and if ye should become over-tipped in wines of vainglorious pride, ye shall remain in Adam and thus continue in the fermenting sin of the bad-fruit wickedness born of our first disobedience. Only through the savior Jesus of Nazareth, the Christ of prophecy, may ye be redeemed, for love resides but where truth has left its mark." And at that, our mother figure thanked him, and we parted and forthwith came upon a wide expanse, and as we trekked this open plain, the rushing wind seemed to speak a dreadful tale for we felt like imprisoned nomads. As we pushed on, we saw in the distance a man walking determinately ahead in our direction, and the youngest with us began to cry, and we quickly hushed her still; but as for the man, there was no sign he saw us; and as we drew closer, and near as we were to him, he went on without seeing us, and aside we moved and let him pass: the eyes of each of us fixed on him—his owl gaze, his gate like warring bones. And after his speck was gone came a plague of demons lashing at our souls like a hostile army upon a helpless village. And the head of us, fearfully bewildered, cried out to Jesus Christ, and flee they did, and all was right. When the fire went up that night, the head of us said, "Keep we should the fire burning until this dark-cloaked land falls to curtained-sleep." And he further said, "What we have witnessed this night, and what the diviner and our mother figure also, should be taken with us." And as he continued about the question of who this Jesus is, the second youngest of us moved to the feet of the mother figure and turned her head and received not anymore, the words of the head of us, but his gesturing body only: for the charade satisfied her more at that hour than much-worded wisdom-talk. And when the fire turned to smoke, and after some rustling, we all went to rest. After daybreak, we came to a marketplace amidst which we came upon a woman of such seeming surety. As this woman approached us, she beheld the head of us and greeted him and gave us meat and said,

"Ye and thy kin are in need of more than what ye have received from me." And at that, the head of us asked her of what she knew of Jesus, and she replied, "The one called Jesus has walked among us; has taught and healed; but many, because of deception and self-promotion, (though they had seen the miracles performed by the one called the son of man through whom the lasting fulfillment of salvation is promised), still yet live by the Law." And after she spoke, we ventured forth and took rest in a barren land, feasting and resting in this desolate place. And before twilight perfected the golden light of day into a most majestic hue, we saw far off a man who seemed to be quite beside himself, a man who when we neared him came toward us raging: the disorder inside him like a dreadful reckoning. When the head of us approached him, he saw that the eyes of the man showed but black and he stood with a disagreeable posture, and, from the crypt of his throat wailed many abominations. And at that, the head of us guided us away; and as we turned to venture forth, we felt a heavy burden. Because of our lack of proper fulfillment, and because the purpose the head of us and the mother figure sought on this journey had not come to its spiritual apogee, we bemoaned much and had little strength to wade through such a deluge of bafflement to reach but the foothill-instruction at the base of the mountain of true knowledge. But on we went like wounded prey and came upon a shrine of golden idols all posed in acts of cruelest action. Such sights took our eyes into downward contemplation. The face of the head of us was emotionally deformed; and the mother of us, her skin turning crimson, struck the idols with stones, and then with seething sounds running from her mouth, eyed the greatest of these in height with the underside of wonder and pushed the heavy idol, and then she fell and tightened and closed her eyes and tears formed like purest diamonds round her lids. We comforted her and soon departed and came upon a man in quite a solemn state, a man whose existence seemed to be but the story of a life having long since been told, for his countenance was a great display of the nature of time. His eyes seemed button-loose upon his well-worn face but showed a fire of rare kindling. And when the father of us reached out his arm to greet this man, the man set his blazoned eyes upon him and took the father of us in like a dream-decipherer, and said, "Those who will not hear the truth will become those whom, by and by will turn the feed of the trough of shame into the stock of a prideful people." He then squinted and departed in his bent to out there somewhere, and at that the mother of us took to pacing not unlike a predatory animal, and the father of us calmed her, whereupon she took to stride with us. And after a time, we came upon a house of mighty squalor, and by the steps of our movements did a woman kneading, hear us, and quickly came to greet us. And out she came with how ashamed she was of her abode and appearance, but at that the head of us neared her and stood beside her with his feelings in his manner and asked her if she could not come out with a story of her living, and she graciously said, "When I was younger and would pace our garden with father, he would take my hand in his and lead me to the place he knew a man called Jesus would be teaching, and not long after, father passed, whereupon I took to know more of the teacher my father believed was the Messiah of Isaiah; and so my manner changed to hearing all I could of him. And after a time, I met a man in dire need who wanted to learn of the Nazarene, but he was bound by his master. One night, whilst dining with my family, amidst the feast I stole myself away from the eyes of the festive drunkenness to the shadowed brush near the agreed upon tower of the fortress built by the conqueror. And when the evening guards lit their torches and began their nightly duty, I was waiting with meat still yet in cheek, and when he came, I kneeled with him and taught him of the Christ, and he wept upon my shoulder, and then I went to my stead and began my nightly worship." At that the mother of us went to rest, and the rest of us engaged each other in a most tightly woven manner: we talked of truth and of the cost of many deeds, each of us making our answers from our hearts, and formed we did our questions from the same. The father of us sat there seemingly pondering the gravest state of man, and when he put forth his hand the way he did, it seemed to say that none was right with the world. And when he lifted his head and turned to us and finally spoke, he said, "I feel that the tomb of my destiny has been sealed forever." And at once we all felt his woe and saw that what was upon him was a kind of wakefulness without the evidence of prior rest. And he suddenly stood but seemed frightened of stepping any way. I was dreary and cautious watching the father of us woefully warring with the likes of which I had never seen. And then the father of us leaped forward and buried his hands in the earth and cried out to be cleansed with the fire of truth. After his outpouring, he sat down his frame amongst us and said, "Is not the plague inflicted man, plagued from but his sin?" Is his sin a family sin?" Is his great sin of sins . . . the sin of the choice to be like unto God Himself, the sin that derailed all men from their spiritual birthright, the sin that determined the fall and tainted every seed of every generation thence, the choice that anchored sin into the heart of man? "Tell me, did the first man know not of that which comes through the blood, driving its tide?" Was he locked in privilege from a full truth tell? Tell me: "Do all who are born, though grown from the ancient ancestral seed, having once been cloaked in its innocent budding, carry in the blood the coiling grip of the beguiler?" After the father of us spoke thus, we hushed, and I stilled in hopes that his outpouring would heavy the jug of the hearing of my ear. I in my mind tried to formulate a reason why such a man as him should be so ill, for none would come to reason thus. What sort of sickness is this that went in unto him? Is he, are we, in stride with truth, or is truth the reason we are in stride with everything but it? I was so brimful with shame and self-despair that I stared for some time into the distance and then I went to the father of us, and when he did not respond, I turned my gaze to the sun, feeling the pain of its power, wanting it to blind my eyes and scorch my soul so I would not have to feel my sorrow. When I lowered my head to rest from such strain I began to inwardly ask to be healed of my ache; and then I laid upon the ground and went to sleep and had a dream that I was in a barren land in a solitary country—the feeling I had was one of banishment; and I saw on the ground before me a man cocked in a frightful stare, his body jerkily moving by the constant plucking of a black and bloody mass of fiendish crows; and then I saw the world erode to the world below where I saw in the murky depths of the abyss, amidst the plateaus of bottommost confinement the terrible configurations of true hopelessness, whereupon I woke and saw the frenzy of our party set to journey. And soon enough we departed and came we upon people gathered that seemed beside themselves, but there was a woman amidst them that said something that seemed to go to the heart of the mother of us, for after we parted there seemed a great spill of herself, for she said, "Had those words not come from a tongue of conviction a bowing would there be of the planks of the vessel." We journeyed on, and soon enough a storm began, and we took rest at an inn in a nearby town, but, before we arrived, we met a man in the road proclaiming that what marches forth from the tongue of man unto the multitudes, if he be not tailor-fitted in the robes of the wisdom of the Lord, are the mere utterings of abominations in accordance with demons. And at that the father of us questioned him further and the man said, "Sir, without truth, battling evil is not a battle at all, for not only does the flower need the proper foundation, but it cannot rightly grow from tainted water. All are sinners, but he who cries out to Christ Jesus shall not meet retribution for his transgressions. Like the strike of the staff of an unwieldy shepherd, shall he be perfectly instructed by the grace of His correction. "Sir, know that thy birth-water broke that ye may live in accordance with His will, for life was not given unto man for the purposes of man, nor is the heart of man the door to his destiny." And at that, the head of us said, "Of listens I am more in need, leave me be to sit with what was said, to know my thoughts like molded clay." And so we all turned the matter over in our minds, and, after a short time, the father of us said, "If we have the right to flame up in vainglorious ways, do we have the right to confess our sins on unchaste knees of much irreverent legs?" "Man does not make ample inquiry of himself, for the soul of man is a cavernous darkness in which the tower of pride keeps bound forever the heart in the blindness of desire. For a man would rather play in the darkness than rest in midday mildness. For the heart of man is an evil thing, for it teaches man that it is the teller of ways.

And if one should continue blind to his nature, he will keep open wide the door for all to enter who may." And at that we thanked this man and made our way toward the inn; and after dinner there were many who drank and danced and those who went forth from the inn and went wroth into the night, for many were the temptations of the bed in which many were in want to lie. And that night, we slept unsettled; and when morning dawned, the father of us thanked the innkeeper and off we went a half-day's journey and came to a place like a drop of spilled creation left to exist without rot nor growth of any kind. An unforgiving place where the ways of many had been spoken of by the innkeeper as darkly wicked—the territory of foreign gods worshipped by an unseemly people the likes of which had strayed from the living God and thus went the route of the lower width of the world where demons take their warring instruction from the highest of the fallen. And not long after we had made our camp, we saw a man kneeling and praying, and stalled we our feet; but from the noise we made amidst this barren region did this man take sight of us whereupon we approached, and after having drawn voice-close nigh he turned to the head of us and said, "Wherefore do ye come this way for ye are come upon an accursed region, for I am the last of a people whose blindness was a blindness to thine own wickedness; but I have been ministered to this very day, lo I have been shown my utter hopelessness; and lo before the sun this morning entered its domain of the sky there was much weeping in my soul, much suffering in my spirit. And before the shadows were cast, I confessed the abominations I practiced with my countrymen and have rightly turned to the Lord for reconciliation, for to die with Him and to rise with him unto the promise of eternal life." This man then became silent and with a stormy mind, tinged with the colors of a sun of joy, said to the father of us, "I was born in this region, but to man afar I go, for a flower hath not a coat from the temper of the wind, but a seed may take upon its back to supply a further land." And after he had said those words, the man left our presence, and we departed, and trekked and trekked we did for quite some time and came upon a young man toiling in a field. And when he saw us, into the house of his father he went and came out with more than bread, and made a dinner spread as for important guests, and then went he and pleaded of his father regarding us, and his father made no case against him. The head of us said to the young man's father, "Ye do right by us; but as much as ye have toiled, I cannot my kin and I feast on as much as ye have given, for the day has barely dawned yet upon thy brow has much sweat begun. By thy face and by thy gnarled hands I know the story of thy efforts, for, do I see that thy seed obey ye—they hearken unto thy call. Pleased ye must be, for I have much respect for thy family and for thy giving nature. In ye I see marvelous fellowship; and if we may abode with ye this night, we might be lifted together in conversation and thereby know the more that is granted those after truth. And at that his wife said, "Ye do not need to thank us, for we are blessed to have ye, for the Lord our God is good, and we shall not turn away those who seek after truth. And at that, her husband said, "Yea woman, ye speak true. Thy workmanship of the stitch of thought fastens understanding without a snag." And then the father called us to the feast whereupon we took rest and dined. After the meal, stout with sustenance, the mother of us asked the man whose land we had thankfully come to tread upon, he who replenished our bodies full from labored days of travel, how their God in whose care they housed their souls could be pleased with them without an alter upon thy stead for to gift Him with offerings, and at that the man said, "He requires no sacrifice but the slaughter of his son, lo the Lamb of God paid our debt of sin upon that tree that day at Calvary. All who would believe in Christ would be reconciled to Him, for as the Father kept His Son, likewise is His son the keeper of his sheep. And just when that was said, the father of us said, "I know the sin that darkens my spirit and plagues my soul is as natural to my nature as the ravenousness of a lion in the wilderness. I cannot last the way I am, for my thirst has not been quenched nor has this soil sprouted such as to be a growth from the flow of living waters. Tell me how much growth is there in this life of settled truth." And the man said, "Before I knew the Lord, I thought myself righteous; and there was a time when such deeming lead me to such craftiness that I with the spirit of pride went amply inward with highest inquiry seeking hidden knowledge whereby I saw myself standing under a sky which seemed cast with stars of my own making in which all secret things were but a part of the constellation of my being. And then what seemed an angel approached me and told me of my special destiny, whereupon I heard a small voice that said *Be not enticed by the power of unclean spirits trust in the Lord Jesus Christ and He shall direct thy paths.* And after those words were spoken, I demanded the seeming angel to tell me in the name of Jesus the Christ what was its name and wherefrom he came, whereupon the light of this being turned dark and hissing and sinister things came forth, whereupon I cried out the name of Jesus Christ whereupon it left, and I felt relieved, but also came to anguish, for I knew I had been deceived. I felt for the first time the evil vileness of my sin, and I kneeled and repented and cried out to Jesus Christ to be forgiven and to be granted salvation. Weeks later, I had, one morning, a strong desire to inquire of myself regarding Christ, for it was upon Him that my heart was fixed. And without two steps, or more than a fleeting thought, answered I had been with the pluck of a belief I had never harped. Who I was could not have kept me from who I had become, for fed by truth did I know I was." And then the father of us said, "Of the which ye speak, there is a bone upon which the meat can hold." And the man said, "Except ye know Christ, ye shall be separated eternally from the Father and thus shall be forever with the legions of the damned." And further added, "Do ye know the one of which I speak as was foretold in prophecy, the God-man that walked the earth as you and me, he whom ye may know as Lord and friend?" And the mother of us said, "I know sir of whom ye speak, but do not know him. How does one believe? What is a sign of newness of life?" And the man said, "Yea woman, a rightful question. There was a time when I but wore the garment of belief but could tell ye not of its texture. But today I stand before ye in the grace of our Lord; for had I not come to live in him and him in me, I would take thy question to mine heart with much dismay for want of answers, but it pleases me that ye ask a question of such importance. I am overjoyed for ye to spend a time with me for to know me in the Faith, for would ye then come to know that I am one in truth." And at that the father of us turned to the man and said, "My family, these strangers, this small-numbered lot: They accompany me on a journey to escape this stalking death. For it is from death we seek to escape. They lap from which I drink, and therefore, following me shall they from tainted waters take. And at that, the man said, "Fall ye upon the grace of Jesus Christ, the perfect life ravaged upon that tree to give ye life." And at that, the father of us went away and began to weep. The mother of us prepared our bedding and thanked the family for the spread of bread and meat, and for the feast of hearty meaning, meaning much to our emaciated hearts. In the morning we could barely part, for we were a weary and beaten lot. But we went on, and the sky became a darker hue. We fell to further sorrows and began to look all around, and all of us found our eyes on the hill yonder and saw a man approaching us with gentle strides and strong intention. We all the while remained grievous yet though curious, and when he neared us, we saw a man of even rougher robe than many, and we welcomed him with drink and bread with what we hoped were worthy greetings. And when the last of us greeted him, he raised his head, and his lids the same rose above his eyes, whereupon the father of us drew nearer to him, whereupon he asked us of our travels and what we seek, and the head of us with struggling breath told about how death seemed more than lurking, and of how we have searched for truth to escape such demise, and to this the man said, "The lack of life in thy heart is like a feast without meat. In me shall ye hunger and thirst no more, for whosoever sups with me shall be fed the course of eternal life. The life I hath offered ye, ye do not take, for rebellion writhes within ye. Thy nature is locked in thy blood, thus do ye forsake the sanctified for the sanctimonious proclamation of thyself. The soul of man is not a splendid region, but is irrevocably contaminated, for all are molded in iniquity. All are hopelessly wicked, consumed by evil. Ye are lost, blinded by the darkness in which ye walk. Blind hast thou been all thy days. Ye labor in vain and thus are unable to peacefully rest. Ye tremble in the darkness, for ye are without the blanket of forgiveness that shall cover thy sin. The universe did I speak forth and bloomed for ye a paradise, but disobedience brought forth sin and death, and man's days were set upon the earth. And his ways were also set. Ye hath writhed with hate by thy desires toward the one who willed ye to be. Hell awaits ye; and without me, separated shall ye be from me and cast into outer darkness where ye shall, with thy nature unloosed, wail and writhe in conscious torment, heave and rage in unrestrained wickedness. Repent, and by my power shall ye believe, and thus will thy heart of stone become a heart of flesh. I am the way, the truth, and the life. To believe in me is to believe not in me but the one who sent me." And after he had spoken thus, we knew it was He who had conquered death: the Redeemer, the Restorer. And when the mother of us confessed her sins and cried out for forgiveness, her burdens released like an ocean a thousand years frozen, creating a massive, emotional tide upon the extraordinary expanse of her heart whereupon she fell to the ground and worshipped the Lord. And the father of us—having been broken enough to realize that his will is but a blind, roving chaos stoked but by the fire of pride—kneeled and wept . . . and wept. Our fellow traveler came to know the sin that enslaved him and sat broken like bones in burlap. And my heart sank in me like the mouth of the sea around a sinking ship. My life had been seemingly unfolding without a horizon of betterment, for I had, all my days, disobeyed the one who created me. I had struggled to make my woe diminish by cultivating the soil of my soul with but prideful sediment. I yearn to be lifted like a root from which all things sprout, and to be firmly planted into the pot of truth from which all things bloom. We spent that night in timeless talk of ageless things. Seeded with repentance I was, thus too deeply sewn to be undone from any thread of reluctance. But a season went before I knew I knew the Lord. And when belief came, thus also did the crop of new life, reaping a most remarkable harvest of conviction.

www.ingramcontent.com/pod-product-compliance
Lightning Source LLC
Chambersburg PA
CBHW071725090426
42738CB00009B/1879